"Marita Littauer's secrets to being a successful and satisfied woman are here. If every woman could absorb the truths in this book, they would experience God's liberating love and change the world."

Stephen Arterburn
Founder and CEO, New Life Clinics; Founder, Women of Faith

"As you read Marita Littauer's fascinating stories of the lives of other women, you will be encouraged to think about your own progress toward self-definition. This book can give you a renewed sense of life perspective, a sense of being a person who is a real person, of defining your own uniqueness, and of defining the picture you have of yourself at your future best. Congratulations to Marita for her contribution!"

Dr. Carolyn Warner
Business Leader and National Education Commentator

"Your life journey will be transformed into an exciting and meaningful adventure as you discover the truths within the pages of this delightful book."

Glenna Salsbury, CSP, CPAE
Professional Speaker and Author of *The Art of the Fresh Start*

"From youth to old age, communication styles to personalities, this book opens the hearts and heads of successful women and demonstrates that every woman has what it takes to be the best."

Thelma Wells
Inspirational Speaker, A Woman of God Ministries

"Offering words and wisdom from God, successful women, and her own vast experience, Marita gives direction to women longing for purpose and balance in their lives."

Candy Davison
Women's Ministries Coordinator, Sandy Cove Ministries

"From the time Marita was a child, I knew she had 'what it takes.' She has always been way ahead of the crowd and is a true leader of women today. I celebrate the birth of this book, which will help you get what it takes, wherever you wish to go!"

Florence Littauer
Author and Speaker, CLASS Speakers Inc.

"As a woman of today, Marita Littauer shares steps to help women discover and celebrate the many opportunities to find their path in life."

Betty Southard
Minister of Caring, Crystal Cathedral

"Marita has done it again. Good information, great encouragement, and Marita's own gracious brand of 'Go for it!'"

Jan Silvious
Speaker, Author, Broadcaster

"A thought-provoking view of the past that provides a boost into a more fulfilling future. After reading *You've Got What It Takes* you will not readily take for granted the great privileges and unique opportunities entrusted to this generation of women."

Connie Neal
Speaker, Author, General Editor of the *Spiritual Renewal Bible*

"This book exudes confidence to the reader. Marita has done our homework for us and keeps us on track in this incredible journey of becoming all that we, as women, were meant to be!"

Joanne Wallace
Speaker and Author

MARITA LITTAUER

You've Got What It Takes

BETHANY HOUSE PUBLISHERS
MINNEAPOLIS, MINNESOTA 55438

Published by Bethany House Publishers
A Ministry of Bethany Fellowship International
11400 Hampshire Avenue South
Minneapolis, Minnesota 55438
www.bethanyhouse.com

Printed in the United States of America by
Bethany Press International, Minneapolis, Minnesota 55438

Library of Congress Cataloging-in-Publication Data

Littauer, Marita.
    You've got what it takes : celebrate being a woman today / by Marita Littauer.
      p.   cm.
    ISBN 0–7642–2275–9 (pbk.)
    1. Women—Conduct of life. 2. Women—History. I. Title.
    BJ1610 .L59 2000
    248.8'43—dc21

                                                   99–6613
                                                 CIP
                                                 Rev.

Thanks to:

My husband, Chuck Noon, for your patience while I was writing,
for letting me make your life public, and for your help in developing
the concepts in the Personality chapter. I love you.

My editor, Steve Laube, for your encouragement and enthusiasm
for this project and for your belief in me as an author.

Carolyn Warner for her book *The Last Word*—a book of quotes for,
by, and about women, from which many of the quotes
in this book were found.

My Christian speaking and writing sisters for specifically sharing
their thoughts about womanhood with me.

Everyone on my e-mail list for ongoing support and encouragement,
for reading various stages of the manuscript, for the endless stream
of stories, and especially for the comments, "I felt really affirmed as a
stay-at-home mom" and "I didn't feel guilty for being a career woman."
Your comments helped me know I was hitting the target I'd hoped for.

———————

MARITA LITTAUER is a professional speaker with over twenty years of experience. She is the author of nine books, including *Personality Puzzle* and *Come
As You Are* (with Betty Southard), and president of CLASServices Inc., an
organization that provides resources, training, and promotion for speakers
and authors. Marita and her husband, Chuck Noon, have been married since
1983.

For additional information on Marita Littauer or CLASServices,
please call 800/433-6633 or visit www.classervices.com.

Contents

Preface

I knew almost no one when my husband and I moved to Albuquerque. To meet people and make friends, I looked in the newspaper to learn when various women's groups were meeting. One of the first events I attended stimulated the thoughts that have evolved into this book. The ideas have churned in my mind for several years. They have shaped my life and my way of thinking. They have made me excited about who I am, where I am, and where I can go in my life. I hope they will do the same for you!

Let me tell you more about this book's inception.

The meeting that affected me so much was quite typical for its kind. Thirty or so women had come, looking sharp and professional. Every stage in adulthood seemed to be represented, from just out of college to retired. People were friendly enough. And like most professional women's meetings, there was a featured speaker. It was the speaker and what she said that so profoundly shaped my thinking—though not in the way she intended.

The speaker, a mature woman, blasted the modern media for its unrealistic view of women. Her entire presentation was filled with anger. She was mad at the world, and to support her view she presented slides comparing models with "real" women, such as wrinkled Native American women, wizened by the passage of time and the out-of-doors, plump grand-mother-types, and others whose appearances sharply contrasted the typical media images. Her goal? We women should rise up and bring about change! While her message had some validity, I couldn't get past her anger.

As I sat there, I thought about my Christian view of the world, summarized in Philippians 4:8 NCV: "Think about things that are good and worthy of praise. Think about the things that are true and honorable and right and pure and beautiful and respected." I realized that I see life through a totally different filter. Rather than being angry, I rejoice in the advancements women have made and the freedoms we have today. We have reason to celebrate!

Yes, there are things most of us would want to change if we had a magic wand. But when we look at the past, especially women's place in it, and we look at the present—where we are today—we see that this point in history is the best time to be a woman! Rather than being angry, as Christian women, let us celebrate being a woman today!

Because today we have a choice. We can complain that a glass ceiling still exists that hampers career advancement, or we can celebrate that in the past decade women-owned businesses have increased by 43 percent and now employ over 18.5 million people. We can whine about getting old, or we can make the most of it—celebrating that today's baby boomers can look forward to many more vital years of life than previous generations. We can fuss over the lack of child-care, or we can start a home-based business, as 40.4 million others have done. We can choose to have a career, or like 45 percent of women, we can slow down and simplify. We can celebrate being a woman today!

I believe that this moment in time, the dawn of the new century, is the best time to be a woman! Thirty years ago a woman who went into the work force was looked down upon and pitied. Then an about-face occurred. As few as ten years ago a woman who wanted to stay home with her children was scoffed at, and her self-worth suffered as a result of her choice. But today women have freedom.

I am one of those modern women, a baby boomer who has taken advantage of the rich opportunities available to women today. I have chosen to be married (sixteen years), but together we have made a choice not to have children—one of those options available to women today. I own a business (CLASServices Inc.) with several employees, another of today's options.

While many of my personal choices are considered non-traditional—especially in a historical context—most of my friends have taken the more conventional path, as have most of the women I speak to and who attend our training seminars. So my life includes many different influences and alternatives. My goal in writing *You've Got What It Takes* is not to push you in one direction or another, but to encourage, motivate, and equip you to see your available options and to make the right choice for your personality, skills, and place in life.

"Celebrate. Life is a never ending exploration of the mind, the spirit, the soul."

MONIQUE MOORE, WRITER

As you read through the pages of this book, gaining a sense of our history as women and being inspired by stories of women both past and present, I hope you will embrace this sense of celebration and be empowered by the knowledge that like so many before you, you've got what it takes!

Celebrate the Present

Looking Back, Moving Forward

Chapter 1

- *Can you imagine what it would be like not knowing how to read? How about not even being allowed to learn how to read?*

- *What about having to marry a man chosen for you by someone else; someone you may never have met, let alone love? What if after your wedding you had to sleep first with the landlord? Imagine trying to start a family and being told by the church when you could or could not have intercourse with your husband.*

- *Picture your activities restricted to the point where you could not go out in public or meet with your girlfriends—let alone have a career, serve in your church, or participate in politics.*

- *Suppose you were not allowed to wear jewelry or own property. Even if your husband, who owned the property upon which you lived, died, you would lose control of the land and your children. By law, your offspring would go to the male members of his family.*

- *Can you imagine being ridiculed, reprimanded, or rejected simply because of your personality?*

While these situations may sound totally unreasonable

today, they were at one time standards of society, from as long ago as ancient Greece and the Middle Ages to as recent as our lifetime! Looking back shows us how far we have moved forward. Taking a brief look at women's history confirms that now is the best time in history to be a woman in America. When we know about the past, we can celebrate the present!

Reading and Education

At the end of a long day one of my favorite things to do is to take a long, hot bubble bath and read. I make good use of my time by going through mail-order catalogs. Much of my Christmas shopping is done from the comfort of the bathroom.

"Just the knowledge that a good book is awaiting one at the end of a long day makes the day happier."

KATHLEEN NORRIS, AUTHOR

When it's time for bed I always read. It might be my Bible, a novel, or another catalog. To get me to quit reading and go to sleep, my husband usually resorts to turning out the light, often while I am mid-sentence. I read up to six books a month. Admittedly, most of them are fiction—leisure reading—but I love to read. I know I am not alone; research indicates that most book buyers are women. Indeed, 77 percent of Christian bookstore customers are women.[1]

If you had been born in ancient Greece, however, chances are you would not be able to read this book—even if it were written in Greek. In those days literacy was a privilege. Most girls learned domestic skills from their mothers, and education beyond that was not needed for the average person. In the Middle Ages, education was virtually inaccessible to women

except for those of noble birth. Their learning typically took place with nuns in convents, and the popular thinking was that only those destined to be nuns should be educated. In 1250 Philippe de Navarre's treatise on conduct advised that women, other than those who would become nuns, should not learn to read because they might encounter love letters that contained indecent language![2] (If women could not read, I do wonder to whom those love letters were intended!)

> "*Learning . . . should be a joy and full of excitement. It is life's greatest adventure; it is an illustrated excursion into the mind of noble and learned men, not a conducted tour through a jail.*"
>
> TAYLOR CALDWELL, BRITISH AND AMERICAN AUTHOR

In sixteenth-century Europe, philosophical discussions began to address a woman's intellect. Girls' education gained consideration. However, since most girls married young and were thrust into household responsibilities, they had little opportunity for education—even if it were available. Those who did not marry young were still not offered an education. They could not hold any public position for which education would equip them, so it was believed they did not need it.

With the invention of the printing press in the mid-1400s and the Protestant Reformation in the early 1500s, women began to be encouraged to learn to read so they could read Scripture. If a woman was taught to read, however, she usually was not taught to write since she "would not be called upon to record events in the family Bible, keep the business's accounts, or maintain any correspondence."[3] Convents were still the primary means of education for women of lesser means. Nobility or the privileged could hire private tutors. *The Timetable of Women's History* says of this period, "While most people still thought of educated women as oddities, unnatural and not quite feminine, the evidence that women were as fully capable as men of sophisticated thought was growing."[4]

During this time (1400s–1500s), many changes occurred in the education of women. Reading and writing became more commonplace, though they were still the exception rather than the rule. In 1486 the first book written by a woman appeared in print. *Book of St. Albans* was authored by British noblewoman Juliana Bemwers. Starting in 1485 Lady Margaret Beaufort, mother of King Henry VII, founded and supported many academic and religious institutions, wrote books, and lectured. In 1528 Baldassare Castiglione wrote *The Courtier*, a book that promoted education and literacy for women, and women's participation in artistic, literary, and musical activities became more acceptable.

> *"The more we know, the more we want to know; when we know enough, we know how much we do not know."*
>
> CAROL ORLOCK,
> NOVELIST AND POET

From this time on the literacy- and education-related accomplishments of women become too numerable to list but do include some interesting facts. In 1709 Susanna Wesley (mother of the Methodist Church founder John Wesley) taught her children and other local children. She offended the local clergy by writing religious textbooks and holding services for the children.[5] In 1750 Maria Gaetana Agnesi, known for her expertise in analytic geometry, was named honorary professor of mathematics at the University of Bologna. Despite this honor she was never allowed to lecture at the university.[6] In 1789 Hannah More began teaching children of miners in western England how to read. She and her sisters also taught them the Scriptures—becoming one of the first Sunday schools in England. However, in those days educating the poor was believed to destroy their interest in farming and other menial tasks. As a result, Hannah and her sisters were condemned and persecuted by church curates.[7]

In 1818 American Emma Willard sought taxpayer support for young women's education. Her written proposal, "An Address to the Public: Proposing a Plan for Improving Female Education," was turned down several times by various cities before the city of Troy, New York, agreed to provide four thousand dollars to fund the Troy Female Seminary. There women could receive a full course of subjects comparable to those offered at the best men's schools. In 1833 Oberlin College was chartered as the first college to admit both men and women, although for the most part the women were in the "female department" and took the "ladies' course." The first female to finish the "full course" graduated in 1841.[8]

Being a speaker and author, I was particularly interested to learn about Fanny Wright, who in 1829 became the first female public speaker and author in America.[9] I am grateful that today women can read, write, speak in public, and get an

> *"I empathize with those who yearn for a simpler world, for some bygone golden age of domestic and international tranquillity. Perhaps for a few people at some point in history there was such an age. But for the mass of humanity it is an age that never was."*
>
> SHIRLEY HUFSTEDLER, FEDERAL GOVERNMENT OFFICIAL

education. This is a present worth celebrating!

Love and Marriage

In my teens and early twenties I dated mostly older men, usually entrepreneurs or salesmen who were successful and well off. My theory was that I was dating for a good time, not to fall in love and find a husband. Men with more money could treat me to the better things in life. I remember my father calling me a gold digger, to which I quipped, "That is because you raised me to expect the best."

When I finally fell in love at the age of twenty-four it was with someone who did not fit the typical profile of men I dated—none of whom I ever fell in love with. Chuck was only three years older than I was. He was in the military and did not have a business background or interest. Since he was so far from my norm, my friends knew something was up when I went out with him more than three times. Five months later we were married. Sixteen years later we are still married, happily most of the time.

I had complete freedom regarding dating and marriage, but this was not always the case for women. In the ancient world, parents arranged marriages. Upper-class marriages were often politically or financially motivated.

I recently saw my sister's family participate in a local production of *Fiddler on the Roof*. I knew the basic story line—times are changing, a fact the Jewish father faces as each daughter rejects tradition and the matchmaker's choice and instead marries for love. The matchmaker's selections are based on which man will be the best provider for the family. My nephew Jonathan played the rabbi's son. When a male student, an outsider, questions the tradition, the son exclaims, "A young girl decides for herself? He's a radical!" Picking one's own mate was considered radical.

Ancient Hebrew law required women to be virgins when they married. Assyrian women could not be seen unveiled in public. Men, on the other hand, were not punished for their sexual activities, and visiting prostitutes was accepted. The husband alone could decide upon a divorce.[10] The Saxon and Thuringian legal codes in about A.D. 800 required that if a free woman married without consent of her guardian, she lost all claims to her property.

Whether a woman married the man her parents picked for her or one of her own choosing, she still had little say about her personal or marital life. In 1140 it was said that "woman's authority is nil; let her in all things be subject to the rule of man . . . neither can she teach, nor be a witness, nor give a guarantee, nor sit in judgment."[11] The Lord's Right of the First Night, established in Scotland by Ewen III, gave property lords the right to deflower the new brides of their retainers and serfs. The husband was declared blasphemous if he consummated his marriage within three days of the wedding, and those who

> "The past which is so presump-tuously brought forward as a precedent for the present, was itself founded on some past that went before it."
>
> MADAME DE STAËL,
> FRENCH AUTHOR

deflowered their bride before the lord had his turn faced legal penalties.[12] (This law plays a part in the 1995 movie *Braveheart*, which is set in the Middle Ages.)

In medieval times the church decided when married couples could have sex—and then only allowed it for procreation because it distracted from spirituality! Sex was not allowed during menstruation, pregnancy, nursing, before or after Communion, and at other times in the liturgical calendar. (Furthermore, according to the Council of Vienne in 1312, women were not allowed to take Communion if they were menstruating or pregnant.[13]) In a time when it was desirable to have many children because they were needed to work the land, most couples who followed the restrictions might have had sex no more than twice a week.

For a clue about what women endured centuries ago, picture being stuck with the boy your parents thought was cute back in junior high school. Imagine your parents and the church rulers involved in your marriage on a daily basis. No wonder so many women entered convents! They provided an alternative to marriage. In the present, we can celebrate our freedom in our marital selections—even to marry or not.

Public Activities and Restrictions

I've heard people say something like "I don't want a cell

phone because I don't want people to be able to find me all the time." Since I'm not always part of the conversation, I keep quiet, but I think to myself, *You can turn off the cell phone.*

That's what I do. I have a cell phone, but you'd be hard pressed to catch me on it. I use it only when absolutely necessary—if I'm lost and need directions, running late, or need to check in at home or with the office. Sometimes it just feels good to be out and about with no interruptions and to be unaccountable. Not that I'm doing anything wrong, mind you! I just like the freedom of saying, "I'm going, and I'll be back in a while." I do not have to report where I've been or what I've done.

Most of us share this freedom. It is something we take for granted. But what if you did not have that luxury?

My friend, speaker and author Donna Partow, knows what it's like to live without freedom—even in the United States. She met, fell in love with, and married an Iranian. Though he was a Christian and they met and lived in America, he retained his traditional Middle Eastern

> *"Knowledge of [another] culture should sharpen our ability to scrutinize more steadily, to appreciate more lovingly, our own."*
>
> MARGARET MEAD, ANTHROPOLOGIST AND WRITER

ways of thinking. For the first ten years of their marriage, Donna was virtually a prisoner in her own home. She was not even allowed to go for a walk around the block or go to the grocery store alone. (I wouldn't mind giving up the grocery store, but I'd surely balk at the rest!) You'd have to read Donna's book *Walking in Total God-Confidence* (Bethany House

Publishers) or hear her speak to get the whole story, but you can be sure that today Donna has a whole new appreciation for going to the grocery store!

While situations like this do occur here in the "land of the free," gratefully they are not the norm. Nevertheless, for our sisters who came before us, control over women and their activities was the rule. Many ancient cultures kept women secluded or under control. Early Jewish societies placed women in a clearly subordinate position. A young girl would be raised under the strict rule of her father. Upon marriage, that authority passed on to her husband—whom she referred to as "master." Women were to keep their heads covered outside the home. Some rabbis even instructed women to be covered within the home, resulting in their children never seeing them. Rabbinical writings indicate leaders of the day frowned upon any public life for a woman.

Although Greek mythology is full of stories of strong women, the average Greek woman's life was that of subservience and seclusion. In the third century women could be involved in various areas of ministry as long as the activities took place in their homes. Jeanne of Navarre, mother of King Henry IV of France, converted to Protestantism from Catholicism, the prevalent religion of the day. Her husband opposed her conversion and imprisoned her in their home as punishment.[14]

The Reformation gave women more freedoms, but nothing like what we enjoy today. Martin Luther and most of his contemporaries believed women to be spiritually weaker than men and therefore subject to their control. Even so, women could participate in their own spiritual growth, reading the Bible and prayer books and conducting services in their home for family members.[15] In the mid-1600s, Margaret Fell Fox, wife of the founder of the Quaker movement, George Fox, organized women's meetings, which allowed women to be a part of the greater service to God. They studied Scripture and were involved in traditional female activities and helpful ministries. The meetings weren't forbidden, but they were hardly accepted by men, who considered the meetings practically equal to women preaching. Just the fact that they were meeting without male supervision drew criticism![16]

> *"If you don't remember history accurately, how can you learn?"*
>
> MAYA LIN, ARCHITECT

Women were excluded from early missionary service. Yes, a woman could accompany her husband to faraway places, but her role was to bear children and take care of her husband. She was not recognized as a missionary nor expected to have a ministry. Accounts of early missionary travels mention little or nothing of the wives' work. Many missionary agencies simply listed the man's name with an "m" after it to indicate he was married. It wasn't until the early 1800s that women were encouraged to be involved in mission work through raising funds and other benevolent activities. By 1929, however, 67 percent of all missionaries from North America were women.[17]

With male/female ratios in modern churches heavily favoring women, it is hard to imagine that at one time women were kept from any type of service in the church or mission field. As we look back, we can see how far we have moved forward. Our ability to come and go, to meet, study, and teach is something worthy of celebration!

Ownership and Control

A few days ago I was looking for a pair of earrings. It had been a while since I had worn that particular pair, so my search expanded to more than one location. I found rings I had nearly forgotten about, cute pins I needed to get out and wear again, and a couple of watches that needed new batteries.

Had I grown up in Rome two hundred years before the birth of Christ, I would have had to fight for the right to wear any jewelry. At that time Roman women marched to urge senators to repeal the Oppian Law. This law, instated for economic reasons during times of war but still in effect years later, forbade women to wear jewels and purple or gold embroidery and from driving carriages. The law was repealed with the argument: "Give the women their baubles; these will satisfy their trivial minds and keep them from interfering in more serious matters."[18]

Restricting the wearing of jewelry and embroidery hardly seems worthy of marching on the senate. If it were the only restriction women faced, they might have accepted it more

> *"Modern invention has banished the spinning wheel, and the same law of progress makes the women of today a different woman from her grandmother."*
>
> SUSAN B. ANTHONY, SUFFRAGIST

graciously, but women were also not allowed to own or inherit property in the ancient world. Even if a woman's husband died, she could not acquire his property. Hundreds of years later, in 1691, Margaret Brent became the first woman on record to own property in the colony of Maryland. In America, "women had greater rights. . . . They could conduct business on their own, under certain conditions, and widows were far more likely to inherit land and other property."[19] Today American women control one-third of the nation's wealth, much of it due to inheritance.[20]

"I've never felt that I was held back because I was a woman. That doesn't mean that everyone has had this experience—in some ways I simply lucked out."

JEANNE M. HOLM,
BRIGADIER GENERAL

I cannot imagine living in a time and place in which women were not allowed to own property. I love houses and real estate. When Chuck and I look at houses, if I see one that needs me, I feel compelled to fix it. I am not co-dependent on people. People are perfectly capable of taking care of themselves and getting their act together. But houses are another story. My husband does not share my compulsion, so it is kept in check.

I was twenty years old and living at home rent-free when I bought my first piece of real estate—a condominium that I rented out and eventually lived in when we first got married. Since then, I've owned several other properties, either individually or jointly with my husband. A goal of mine is to someday have both the time and money to buy houses that are structurally sound but need TLC. I'd love to fix them up and make them salable or rentable.

Not only were ancient women prohibited from owning or inheriting property, if a woman's husband died, she also lost her own children! In A.D. 780 the Saxon legal code prevented women from assuming guardianship of their children. Instead, male kinsmen, preferably married, took that responsibility.[21] How times have changed. My husband worked as a social worker for several years. In a case of death or divorce, children almost always go to the mother or her family. The prevailing thought: Mothers know best. Something more to celebrate today!

Rejection and Acceptance

Obviously had I lived in a different era I would have had a tough time. My guess is that you would have too! Even if I could be content without reading (after all, ignorance is bliss); even if I liked that guy from junior high enough to marry him; and even if I did not care about owning anything, I still would have had trouble. My God-given personality would have been unacceptable to much of society.

I've been described as outgoing, loud, talkative, and energetic. Had I lived in an earlier time, I would have had to constantly hide who I was or become a social outcast. Mary Todd Lincoln, for instance, was institutionalized briefly, in part, because of her strong personality. She was described as "an intelligent, aggressive, strong-willed and outspoken woman in a day when the general public had little tolerance for women of that character."[22] Eleanor Roosevelt, at the time of her husband's presidency, was sharply criticized for the same type of personality. People thought she was too strong, a rebel. Today many women hold her up as a role model, and her outspoken words are often quoted. In contrast, Jackie Kennedy was adored by the public. She looked like a doll and kept her mouth shut. Jackie fit the public's image of a president's wife. Imagine how Hillary Clinton would have been received if she had been married to Abraham Lincoln!

As recently as 1972 TV news anchor Leslie Stahl got in trouble for smiling. When she first started out in the business, she was pulled aside and told not to smile. Men could smile but women could not because they had to try harder to convey authority![23] Things surely have changed. One of our local news stations has even stepped away from the traditional male/female combo for the nightly news and is now anchored by two women. Women are free to be who God made them to be. They no longer need to look or act like men to be successful.

When we look back we can see how far we have advanced. Virtually every area of our female lives has been touched—education and literacy; romance and marriage; public presence; property ownership; even our personalities. While I have taken you on a quick hopscotch approach through women's history, I hope it has opened your eyes to how blessed we are today. Yes, I have pulled out some isolated cases in history; I have selected facts that seem laughable by today's standards, but they are an accurate representation of past times.

Certainly yesteryear's women accomplished notable feats, and queens were great leaders. But these outstanding women were the rare ones, the unusual. Today outstanding women are the usual. Hundreds of amazing stories could be told. I hope this quick taste of history has prompted you to want to learn more. As we look back, we see that now is indeed the best of times for women. Today we can have purpose, passion, power, and privilege! Whatever you want to do, whoever you want to be, today you've got what it takes!

Celebrate the Privileges

Making Choices That Are Right for Your Life

Chapter 2

Today's women
Born yesterday
Dealing with tomorrow;
Not yet where we're going
But not still where we were.

ADRIENNE RICH, POET AND EDUCATOR

Within months of each other Heather Wilson and Brenda Barnes received national attention. Their feats were noteworthy because they represented views from opposing, or at least differing, spectrums, yet both were applauded.

In case you missed Heather's and Brenda's moments in time, let me briefly tell you about these women.

As I started to write this book, Heather Wilson was elected to the U.S. Congress. That in itself is hardly noteworthy; women have been in national politics since 1916 when Jeanette Rankin was the first woman elected to Congress. What makes Heather unique (other than serving my hometown of Albuquerque and receiving my vote) is that she is the first female military veteran to serve in Congress. Heather's military career began at the Air Force Academy, which did not

"As women today, we face a smorgasbord of opportunities. Gradually, we are coming to understand that the variety of options before us doesn't require us to respond with an all-at-once mentality. The previous panic that propelled us to line up plate after plate on our cafeteria trays because 'we might not ever get a chance again' is being replaced by a peace that we can select the best option for our current life situation.

"That we can take only a few selections from a whole line of 'desserts' means we have developed a sense of discipline and a respect for the health of limitations.

"How I rejoice in this sanity! Now . . . to put back a few of the goodies I thought I just had to have."

ELISA MORGAN, PRESIDENT OF MOPS INTERNATIONAL

allow women to attend until 1976. Interestingly, she is also the first Air Force Academy graduate—male or female—to be elected to Congress.[1]

Heather Wilson was a "first" in the 1990s. However, the last two decades have seen a burst of firsts for women—especially in the area of careers and work. American women have been active in the work force since the Industrial Revolution in the late nineteenth century, but working women really gained the spotlight in the 1980s as women began to move into high-ranking positions. In 1981 Sandra Day O'Connor was the first woman appointed to the U.S. Supreme Court. In 1983 Sally Ride became the first woman to travel in space. And in 1984 Geraldine Ferraro was selected as the Democratic Party's vice presidential candidate—the first female to receive such an honor in either party.

With this popularization of working women, those who chose to stay home and take care of their husbands and raise their children were looked down upon. After all, the National Women's Conference in 1977 drew up a 25-point plan designed to help women achieve future goals in a variety of areas, including education, health insurance, and eliminating discrimination. Women like Sandra Day O'Connor, Sally Ride, and Geraldine Ferraro were certainly attaining these goals.

Women who weren't making history, or at least climbing the corporate ladder, were made to feel inferior. Rosa Jordan of Saginaw, Texas, told me that her friends at work thought she was crazy for staying home with her children after climbing her way up from an entry-level job to a supervisory position. Judy Shortt of Hillsboro, Oregon, adds, "Ten years ago, if you didn't want to pursue the most exciting, upwardly mobile occupations, and instead wanted to 'just' mother and volunteer, well, you didn't have vision."

Women who chose to stay home and be moms were disparaged in the '80s. But today Brenda Barnes has become the poster child for this school of thought—making staying at home okay, giving women the option of a choice. In October 1997 the business world was shocked by Brenda's decision to stay home with her children. The media was filled with stories and commentaries like this one from the *Sacramento Bee*:

By this new standard, Brenda Barnes, who just quit a top job at PepsiCo, is a heretic. *The Wall Street Journal* recently called her "one of the highest-ranking women in corporate America," and headhunters were predicting that she would be on the short list to be CEO of any number of big companies.

Yet last month, Barnes renounced it all to spend more time with her family. She had faithfully devoted 22 years to her work, and now—to everyone's shock— she is choosing the company of her husband and children, ages 7, 8 and 10, to that of her secretary, her computer, and her boss.

With our new theology still in its infancy, we have no idea what to do with these corporate surprises. Can we bemoan the glass ceiling, celebrate women who break through it, and at the same time applaud those who choose to return to a more traditional role?

Yes, our culture should be able to honor all those choices at once. But human beings prefer not to have to deal with paradoxes, contradictory truths and conflicting trends. We'd better get used to it, though, because come the next millennium, we are going to see both more women in top jobs and more women— and men—deciding to put family rather than career first.

Opportunities

As I work with women all over the country, I find that the world had better get used to more and more women making choices based on what is right for their lives and families rather than what popular media tells us we should be doing. How exciting! As Jo Hancock told me,

> After being a partner in a law firm and then going out on my own as a sole practitioner, I knew I needed to be available for my teenager, Brooke. I closed my law office at a time that it was becoming well established and went home to be available for Brooke when she was 13 years old. I am so glad I had the opportunity to do that.

"Instead of looking at life as a narrowing funnel, we can see it ever widening to choose the things we want to do, then take the wisdom we've learned and create something."

LIZ CARPENTER, AUTHOR

There are so many opportunities, options, and advantages for women today. We have what it takes!

Career options are just one of the many privileges we women have today. Yes, many areas of society still need improvement. Many working women contend with a glass ceiling, and though numbers vary depending on the survey, it is fairly widely accepted that women still don't receive equal pay as men. The average female worker in America earns just seventy-six cents for every dollar a man earns, up seventeen cents from the 1970s.[2] Only 11 percent of Fortune 500 companies have female officers.[3] We can choose to focus on these discrepancies, or we can see the flip side and celebrate that this is the best time in the history of the world to be a woman.

"This has got to be one of the most exciting times to be alive and be a woman. Many of the diseases that killed us and our children in years gone by have been conquered by medicine. The doors to many of the careers that were closed to us have swung wide open—or are at least open a crack. We are no longer considered expendable commodities as we were when our immigrant ancestors came to this country. It was the practice at the time to put women and children in the most dangerous places in the factories because they really didn't count much. Today, women are running similar factories and are enormously successful.

"I am glad to be a woman today. I'm glad I've had opportunity after opportunity offered to me. And I'm glad I stepped through those open doors and now have a career that is fulfilling because it meets my financial needs and most of all because my work is a ministry to others. I am glad that I have value and worth in my company."

GWEN ELLIS, SPEAKER AND AUTHOR

As a Christian, I believe we should apply Philippians 4:8 NCV to our outlook: "Sisters, think about the things that are good and worthy of praise. Think about the things that are true and honorable and right and pure and beautiful and respected." When we set our sights on the good, the right, and the respected, we see that we have many things to celebrate.

Looking at the good in life, we can applaud women in business. Women are starting businesses in record numbers. Government statistics reiterate the fact that women are among the fastest-growing groups of small business owners.[4] From 1972 to 1995 the number of women-owned businesses increased from 5 percent of all businesses to

35 percent. They now contribute more than $1.6 trillion to the national economy and employ more people than Fortune 500 companies.[5] Another report says women-owned businesses grew 43 percent between the 1980s and the 1990s.[6] While these are typically small businesses (very few women-owned businesses report sales that come close to those posted by Fortune 500 companies), combined they are making a big impact on the economy.[7] Smaller businesses tend to give today's women the freedom and flexibility they desire, usually not available from corporate America.

Mary Ann Remnet is one of many women who appreciate the flexibility of a small business. She says,

As a female business owner, I sculpt my time to work with other women whose lives have gotten out of balance.

My children are now sixteen and eighteen. Being self-employed in a home-based business, I am able to serve on (among other things) the parent advisory board at San Diego State University where my daughter goes to school. We are currently working on the establishment of a Leadership Center that will serve as a model for similar programs at other schools. As a Christian woman, it pleases me to help shape such a key program at a secular university (the largest school in the State university system).

By owning my own business, I also have time to work with the young Hispanic girls in Ventura County,

YOU'VE GOT WHAT IT TAKES

where I live, through a program with an organization called City Impact. Their "Las Angelitas" mentor program matches mild to high risk kids with businesswomen in the community to help them get (or stay) on track.

Women today can choose to be whatever they want to be. Several years ago my nieces were visiting me and a girl who lived nearby came over to play with them. I asked each what she wanted to be when she grew up. Their answers perfectly matched their personalities.

One niece quietly said, "I want to be, you know, someone who stays home with the kids."

"A mom and a housewife?" I asked.

She nodded.

The girl down the street proudly said, "I want to be a professional baseball player or a bank president."

Someday my niece may have that opportunity to be a stay-at-home mom. And though the girl down the street may never be a professional baseball player, many women are bank presidents. A recent survey revealed that 50 percent of females between the ages of eighteen and thirty-four want a world where they can choose to be anything—president of the United States or a mother, or both.[8] The choice is ours.

I do not recall having the typical childhood dreams of being a ballerina, nurse, or teacher. But I do know that being a woman never influenced my plans. I started my own business when I was only nineteen. At that time I didn't tell people my age because I was afraid people wouldn't consider me credible. That first business, color analysis, evolved into my being a full-time professional speaker and writer. Now in my forties, I freely tell my age. I have remained self-employed throughout my adult life and now own CLASServices Inc., a service agency

> *"I am not held captive to decisions I made ten, twenty, thirty years ago; I can grow, change, start over, begin anew."*
>
> BETTY SOUTHARD,
> SPEAKER AND AUTHOR

that offers resources, training, and promotion to Christian speakers, authors, and publishers. I had no childhood dreams of becoming what I am today, but I also had nothing holding me back.

Susan O'Malley was thirteen when she was assigned the school paper we all had: What do you want to do when you grow up? Susan wrote that she wanted to run a professional sports franchise. Her teacher's response? "Good composition, unrealistic goal." Despite the lack of encouragement, two decades later Susan is the top-ranking woman executive in team sports as president of Washington Sports, which runs the business side of the Washington Capitals and Washington Bullets.[9]

Who knows where my mother would be if she had been born thirty years later. When her life was in its shaping stages, she did not have the opportunities we have today. While she has always had a love for politics, she became a teacher. Women in the 1940s did not aim for a political life. Today she is still a teacher of sorts, traveling all over the world teaching people through her speaking and writing. As I write these words, she is scheduled to leave in a few days to speak in Austria. She is very successful—having written over thirty books, she has received international acclaim. Yet she still talks about politics and jokes that when she settles down she may run for a local office in the retirement area of Palm Springs, where she lives. "After all," she says, "here I am still young!"

Many women have chosen to take the corporate route. Some have decided to go into politics. Plenty of women have started small businesses. Others, like Brenda Barnes, have chosen to stay home with their children. Still others have selected a combination that fits their individual lifestyle.

Many mothers who want to spend more time with their children are opting for what has been called voluntary simplicity—spending more time with family and friends, reducing stress, and doing more to make a difference in their communities, usually resulting in making less money. Research indicates that thirty- to forty-year-old middle class women are making this change more than any other group, and they are overwhelmingly happy about their choice.[10] Speaking of her own life, Judy Shortt said,

> I think we are beginning to embrace and create time to slow down. We are finding time to enjoy the simple pleasures of friends and tea, or children and a movie, or a husband and a weekend. As I age, I am beginning to place more value on these interludes

sandwiched between more "ambitious" endeavors. I am finding these quiet times are taking on a new significance in my life.

I particularly like what *Executive Female* magazine called "A Life Worth Living," which involves striking a balance between career ambition, free time, keeping up with friends, fulfilling creative potential, and so on.[11] I read this article at a time in my life when some changes were needed. I had been living in Southern California, working long hours, and speaking around the country on weekends. The frenetic pace was taking a

> *"You know, your career is just your career. Your life is your life!"*
>
> SISSY SPACEK, ACTRESS

toll on my mental health and my marriage. I felt my inner being crying out for a yearlong retreat.

Little did I really expect to get it. However, before discussing my need for a change with my husband, he was offered a job in Carlsbad, New Mexico—vastly different from Southern California, as you can imagine.

We moved from a lovely executive home to a small bungalow. Southern California has too many area codes to count—and they keep changing. New Mexico has one—for the entire state. Freeways crisscross Southern California. New Mexico has three, and the closest one to Carlsbad is three hours away—in Texas. We lived in Carlsbad exactly one year before moving to the intersection of New Mexico's two biggest freeways, Albuquerque. I got the yearlong retreat I needed and now have a life shaped into one "worth living."

Whether you work in corporate America, start a small business, combine work and personal life, or stay home with your kids—the choice is yours. These varied opportunities may be why home economics, now called family and consumer sciences, is making a comeback. Education professor Wanda Fox says,

> For a while society placed less value on family life and became very career—and business—oriented. Now we're realizing that we need both. These classes focus on decision making skills, career planning, consumer economics and balancing work and family.[12]

No longer does culture dictate which direction you should go. This is a privilege worth celebrating!

Options

Remember being in first or second grade? Didn't your teacher seem old?

When we were very young, all adults seemed old—our parents, teachers, especially our grandmothers! My grandmother was a lovely, gentle woman. She did not work outside the home. She often stayed with us kids while my parents traveled. We'd sit in her lap while she read us stories. She tried to teach me to play the violin and to knit and crochet. Other times we'd go to her apartment for pot roast or New England boiled dinner. She was a good grandmother, doing grandmotherlike things. But she seemed so old, and not very active.

When I look back at photos and do some basic math, I realize she really wasn't that old. My most vivid memories are when she was in her late fifties and early sixties. Then again, that was considered old back then. It wasn't just my childhood perception! You were old at fifty and you "dressed your age."

> *"The process of maturing is an art to be learned, an effort to be sustained. By the age of fifty you have made yourself what you are, and if it is good, it is better than our youth."*
>
> MARYA MANNES, JOURNALIST

Our numerical age is far less important these days. With a young attitude we can be virtually any "age" we want, as long as we have our health. The choice is ours. I think this e-mail I received accurately represents how we've changed our aging attitudes:

> In the not too distant past,
> I remember very well Grandma baking,
> cooking, sewing and handing out advice.
> She no longer waits for us to come
> to taste the cookies in the jar
> or try on the latest slippers she made
> or sample pudding made from rice.
> But Grandma hasn't deserted you,
> she's just learned something new;
> in fact, if you want to chat with her

you'll find her in ICQ!
She's scanned your photos
and your artwork too,
and proudly sends them around;
and now she sees you daily
as she's installed you as "background."
She's out now with her "puter" pals,
sharing links and URLs.
You still call her Grandma
but she's known as "Giga-Gal."
Grandma's joined the electronic age,
and it really seems to suit her.
So don't expect the same old gal,
'cause Grandma's gone "computer"!

I had to chuckle when I first read this poem. For my mother's seventieth birthday we gave her her first computer. While she still writes all her books in longhand, she has become a whiz at e-mail. She is thrilled because she has learned to change fonts and colors. Of course, I e-mailed her a copy of "Grandma's Gone Computer." Her grandchildren, my nephews, frequently teach her new computer tricks. One day she called me all excited: "My computer plays music!" she exclaimed. They had shown her how to play a music CD on the computer.

Evelyn Kliewer is another grandma gone computer! She says, "As a grandmother I am becoming computer literate . . . first, learning to use the mouse, Windows, etc. Then I mastered software for music. Now I can do multi-track recording. I enjoy making greeting cards. My new computer skills are in addition to traveling and speaking and doing the entire payroll and bookkeeping for our post-retirement business!"

As I remember my grandmother, I can't see her ever learning computers, even if they had been around. She never bonded with the microwave and preferred to reheat leftovers in the oven or on the stove. Today chronological age is virtually irrelevant.

An article in *USA Today* addressed this new agelessness. It highlighted John Glenn going into space at the age of seventy-seven and other seniors doing more than most teenagers. Lenny Aikins is eighty-three, and he parachutes six times a week. Paul Tatum is seventy-six and competes in cross-country cycling. As Paul crossed a finish line, a reporter asked how he felt about old age. His reply: "When I get there, I'll tell you."[13] Anne Colby, director of Radcliffe College's Henry Murray Research Center, says, "There's been such a loosening of social prescriptions for what a woman can do at any given age: A woman who's forty might be running a company or just going back to college; she might be a grandmother or having her first baby."[14] The meaning of the word "old" has truly changed, and it's not just because we are getting older. Age is becoming less and less important universally.

Good Housekeeping magazine featured an article titled "I Don't Feel a Day Over . . ." in which author Pamela Redmond Satran addressed today's different expectations regarding age:

> *"I'm not interested in age. People who tell me their age are silly. You're as old as you feel."*
>
> ELIZABETH ARDEN,
> COSMETICS EXECUTIVE

When my old-world grandmother was in her forties she rolled up her gray hair into a bun, rolled her support hose down to her ankles, put on a housedress and took to her bed with Arthur Godfrey on the radio and a box of Dugan's cupcakes. My mother, at age forty, bought a stronger girdle and a bottle of hair dye. I joined a gym, invested heavily in AHA moisturizers and cranked up my career.[15]

Many of today's well-known celebrities are the age my grandmother was when she was "old." Model and actress Lauren Hutton is fifty-six at the time of this writing. Goldie Hawn, Bette Midler, and Diane Keaton each have their own unique look, but all are nearing their mid-fifties. Jane Fonda is over sixty! Admittedly, each probably has more time and money to spend on looking young than most of us do, but if staying in shape and looking young are important to you, you can do that. There are creams, lotions, and potions for our faces, exercise programs and diets for our bodies, and dressing our age is virtually a thing of the past.

The key phrase here is "If it's important to you . . ." If maintaining your youth is important to you, you have options today. Having recently turned forty, I have chosen to keep myself in the best possible shape. I don't obsess over it, but I try to take care of myself. I have virtually cut sugar out of my diet.

I drink lots of water. I have been using glycolic acid on my face for several years and have recently added retin-A. I play tennis, ride a mountain bike and a motorcycle, and in-line skate. I'm no good at any of them, but I have fun and they help keep me in shape.

"There is a fountain of youth: it is your mind, your talents, the creativity you bring to your life and the lives of the people you love. When you learn to tap this source, you will have truly defeated age."

SOPHIA LOREN,
ITALIAN ACTRESS

Not every woman thinks acting and looking young is important. And that's okay, too! I have friends who are grandmothers and thrilled with their traditional grandma role and place in life. They do not work out. They do not worry about their wrinkles, gray hair, or changed body shape. They are happy as they are. That in itself is a great freedom, a privilege worthy of celebration.

Speaking of body shapes, there's reason today to celebrate this, too. It used to be that women who were bigger or smaller than the norm were out of luck. Larger women resorted to dressing in muumuus. Small women had to take hems up on everything. Today there are special magazines and shops for "big, beautiful women." When actress Camryn Manheim won a Golden Globe Award for her work in *The Practice*, she held the award over her head and said, "This is for the fat girls everywhere." Her "big, beautiful" size has given others like her a new credence and sex appeal. On the other end of the spectrum, there are clothing stores such as Petite Sophisticate and 5–7–9. Something for everyone.

> "*Age is totally unimportant.*
> *The years are really irrelevant.*
> *It's how you cope with them.*"
>
> SHIRLEY LORD, WRITER AND
> MAGAZINE EDITOR

One year I invited Liz Curtis Higgs to speak at the Southern California Women's Retreat. Like Camryn, Liz has given the big and beautiful a voice and acceptability. My good friend Connie Swanson is the emcee for the Southern California Women's Retreat. Connie is very thin, probably wears a size 2. I wear a fairly average size. Everything fits me straight off the rack with no taking in, hemming up, or letting out. At the retreat the three of us got talking about diet and size. Our conclusion: "I eat whatever I want and this is the size I come out." We all laughed, grateful that today, whatever size you are is okay as long as you are healthy and happy with it. What a privilege!

Another option we have is in our clothes. While boarding a recent business flight, one woman in particular caught my eye. She was wearing a pantsuit that seemed to be made of gray pinstripe wool, just like a typical man's suit. She completed her outfit with a white shirt and black shoes. It was the old "dress for success" look for women, which I hadn't seen in a long, long time. I had forgotten how blessed we women are today that we can be in business, be successful, and dress like women! I scanned the rest of the crowd waiting to get on the plane. Many women were obviously professional women on business trips yet they had an updated, professional look; they looked like women—wearing a variety of colors and styles. Even the freedom we have in our wardrobe is a privilege!

"I've just celebrated my fifty-eighth birthday and every birthday seems to get better and better. I've been in the professional speaking business for nearly twenty years and have had some difficult times—bias, prejudice, discrimination. But the last three years have been the very best. Opportunities to speak to thousands, book contracts, a loving husband, supportive children and four precious grandchildren are examples of some of my achievements.

"Why am I so excited about this? Looking back, as a black woman born in adverse circumstances, raised by a great grandmother in the South, with what some people thought were severe strikes against me, I am able to enjoy the success of the abundant life Christ promised in spite of those odds.

"Looking forward, there are absolutely no limits to what I can do with God in charge of my life. I wear a bumblebee pin every day to remind me of that great affirmation in Philippians 4:13 NKJV, 'I can do all things through Christ who strengthens me.' That's why my motto is: In Christ I can BE the best. The only barrier to my continued success is my rejection of the perfect will of God. When I try to do things without allowing His perfect will, I mess up."

THELMA WELLS, SPEAKER AND AUTHOR

Advantages

Yes, we women today have far more opportunities and options than our grandmothers or even our mothers had. We also have advantages. Denise Jardine is one woman who is grateful for these advantages:

I am twenty-nine years old and have had it much better than my mother or grandmother ever did. My mother encouraged me at the age of thirteen "to go to college and make something out of myself." I remember that conversation as if it were yesterday. My parents married when my mom was eighteen and my dad was twenty. It wasn't until after eighteen years of marriage that my mom was able to go to a junior college to receive her certified nursing degree—much to my dad's dismay. At the time my parents were in the process of getting a divorce and my mom needed to go back into the marketplace. She had no job experience except for being a full-time wife, mother, and house manager for over eighteen years. My mom wasn't able to make more than minimum wage. She held down two to three jobs just to pay the bills. I give my mom a lot of credit for raising two teenagers on her own, working for minimum wage, and going to college so she could do something that she would truly enjoy. From her, I learned the importance of going to college.

I, on the other hand, had advantages! I was the

first one in my family to go to a four-year college. During my mother and grandmother's generations, this was not an option for the average person. Soon after graduating, I pursued a Master's degree in Social Work at the University of Illinois in Champaign-Urbana. I graduated and began my first job in a hospice. Thirteen months after starting this job, I was laid off along with six other people due to corporate down-sizing. It was a true blessing in disguise. God soon opened up the doors at my current place of employment. I do social work and marketing for a home health agency. I absolutely love what I do. I enjoy the variety, flexibility, and freedom that I have. I also work with my mom, who is a certified nursing assistant!

I am truly grateful for the opportunities I have had in the workplace and the opportunity to go to college and graduate school. Both of these advantages were new adventures for my generation. I know this change will have a positive impact on future generations to come.

An important advantage that we have today as Christian women is our ability to be involved in leadership and to take a more active role in church. Whether or not you agree with it, many more women teach from the pulpit today. Personally, at this point, I have not filled the pulpit during a main weekend service, but many of my speaker friends have. One of my female cousins is an ordained minister who is the senior pastor

> *"When my grandmother was widowed by a Kentucky coal mining accident in 1923, her few options to support herself and her three youngsters included taking in boarders or rapid remarriage. By contrast my widowhood years later—while still tragic—were eased by my education and the career opportunities allowing me to provide for my two young children."*
>
> SANDRA P. ALDRICH,
> SPEAKER AND AUTHOR

of the church she serves.

Joyce Meyer, whose *Life in the Word* TV program airs on hundreds of local stations, seven cable channels, and seven satellite networks, recently said, "Somebody told me they had been talking to a Baptist minister who really likes my teaching. He said, 'If Joyce Meyer were a man, she'd probably be the best teacher in America today.' "[16] This attitude is slowly changing. Today more and more women are developing speaking platforms.

My mother, Florence Littauer, reflects on her thirty years in Christian ministry:

I am so glad to be a woman in today's society and more importantly to be a Christian woman! While much of the women's movement is in opposition to many biblical principles, the focus on equality has seeped into churches so that male pastors feel they must give women credit and responsibilities.

For me this opening of opportunity came just when I was ready for it. The positive changes in the last thirty years have been amazing. Where I used to be a token in a lineup of dignified scholars, I am now chosen to serve for my abilities and knowledge. Many years ago, a pastor told me he needed to fill out his seminar roster and he chose me as the token female because I wasn't "fluffy or whiney." I have been given the ultimate compliment from men over and over: "What I like about you is that you think like a man."

As time has passed, the acceptance of women in church leadership has grown to the point where now women's ministries are expected in many churches and some are even putting women on the board.

I am so grateful to have been on the forefront of the Christian women's march of progress. Thirty years ago I was a voice crying in the wilderness, where recently I was chosen by men I did not even know to receive a Doctor of Humanities degree [from Southwestern Adventist University]. I've tried to be knowledgeable without being arrogant, feminine without being "fluffy or whiney."

For the Christian women who desire to speak, write, and lead, I hope I have made a wide path in the desert of opportunity. I celebrate being a woman today!

Another advantage Christian women have today are the many resources developed specifically for women. There are various devotional Bibles designed for women; even a study Bible that emphasizes issues of concern or interest to women.

The Woman's Study Bible (published by Thomas Nelson) features biographical sketches of women of the Bible and study notes from a woman's perspective. As I read and study it, I continually find interesting insights within the added information.

One of the most exciting advantages we have as Christian women is the confidence we can have when we know our lives have purpose—when we know that we are where God wants us to be. As Rosa Jordon told me, "It is really about choices and being happy with the ones you have made." Heather Wilson made the choice to pack up her family and move to Washington, D.C., to serve in Congress. Brenda Barnes made the choice to go in the other direction, leaving corporate America to spend more time with her family.

The choice is yours!

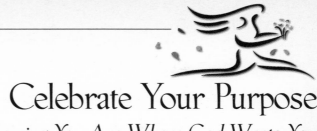

Celebrate Your Purpose
Knowing You Are Where God Wants You
Chapter 3

I suspect there's hardly a person alive who hasn't wished for a crystal ball of sorts. Wouldn't it be great to know what decisions to make? To know what we should be doing in our life or where we'll be in ten years? How much easier everything would be if we always knew the right choice to make. Surely, if we made the right choice we'd be happy with it—that's partly why it's the right choice!

Of course, life doesn't work that way. There are no crystal balls that reveal the true future, though I've heard the 8 Ball from my childhood has had a resurgence of popularity. I remember shaking the black ball, flipping it over, and anxiously waiting for an "answer" to float to the surface. Nowadays computer software is available that walks us through a variety of decision-making situations.

> *"When I stand before God at the end of my life, I would hope that I would not have a single bit of talent left and could say, 'I used everything you gave me.'"*
>
> ERMA BOMBECK,
> HUMORIST AND WRITER

When I look for direction or purpose for my life, I surely do not want to leave it up to a series of random yeses, no's, and maybe's. A computer program might help narrow down and clarify my options, but I still wouldn't leave something as important as the rest of my life up to a machine. At the least, I want divine intervention. What I'd really like is writing in the sky.

At home I often hear voices from the sky. Before reporting me to the authorities, let me explain. Hot air ballooning is very popular in Albuquerque, and many Saturday and Sunday mornings the balloons fly so low over our house that I actually hear the voices of the people aboard—voices from the sky, but certainly not divinely inspired. So where do we go to find God's direction for our lives? How can we truly celebrate our purpose and know that we are where God wants us?

For my own life and that of many others I'll cite, that direction comes not from writing in the sky but from writing that has been there waiting for us forever—from God's Word!

I remember arguing with a pastor friend years ago. He insisted that every answer we needed could be found in God's Word. I agreed in principle but argued that the answers to many of today's problems are not there in black and white. In essence, this was an argument in which we were both right.

Within God's Word are the basic life skills we need. Within God's Word we do find answers or at least the guidance to help us find the answers we need. Yet when I have a specific situation in which I need an answer—should I buy this house or that one; should I take this job or not—the correct response is not listed there in black and white. Still, when we follow the guidance offered to us in God's Word, we find that we *can* make right choices.

Knowing God's purpose for our lives—being where God

wants us—is a wonderful blessing. It helps carry us through difficult times. Obstacles and objections in our path become doable detours rather than roadblocks hindering our progress.

Just today, before leaving the office to come home and write, I faced an obstacle. An employee had let me down by failing to carry out her responsibilities. Instead of being home writing and being creative, I was at the office feeling kicked in the stomach, discussing the problem with the employee's supervisor. *Is this worth it?* I thought to myself. I hate employee problems, and they're certainly not conducive to creative thinking. Many days I feel like I should chuck it all and go sell real estate.

"My childhood was spent in the traditional '50s and turbulent '60s, watching women go from being housewives, teachers, secretaries, and nurses—each one a valid calling—to women in the '70s opting for construction work, mechanical engineering, and lumberjacking, simply to prove we could do it. Girlfriends, we did it and we did it well. In the '80s we made money in law, medicine, and finance; in the '90s we forged families and friendships, but now . . . oh, now come the best years of all! In the twenty-first century we women are making a difference. With our wisdom and resources, we're creating lives full of meaning and purpose, not only for ourselves but for all whom we love and for the Lord we serve. I love being a twenty-first century woman of God!"

LIZ CURTIS HIGGS, BEST-SELLING AUTHOR OF *ONLY ANGELS CAN WING IT, THE REST OF US HAVE TO PRACTICE*

> *"God does not ask your ability or inability. He only asks your availability."*
>
> MARY KAY ASH,
> COSMETICS EXECUTIVE

But I don't. I keep at it because in my heart I believe that I am doing what God wants me to do. I believe that writing this book, and those before and after it, is a part of what God wants me to do. I believe what we are doing at CLASS is what God has prepared me for my whole life. I believe it is my purpose. That strong core guides my decisions and my life. I have the strength to go around obstacles and keep moving forward. So here I am, writing!

When we know God's purpose for our lives, we gather strength. We can celebrate despite difficulties. This divinely inspired drive keeps me and many other women going.

Do you want to know God's purpose for your life in this new century? I hope so. Unfortunately, I can't be the one to tell you God's purpose for your life. And you won't find in the Bible something as concrete as "Susan, do _____ with your life." Nevertheless, it is in the Bible that you will find the steps to help you know God's direction for your life. You can hear His voice guiding you and giving you purpose.

Know God

The first step to knowing God's purpose for your life is to truly know Him. This means more than just believing there is a God out there, a Creator of the universe. Most Americans believe there is a God or a Supreme Being. But having a close personal relationship with Him is so much more than that. Knowing Him starts with inviting Jesus Christ into your life.

I was nine years old when I had my tonsils out. When I was in the hospital my father talked to me about inviting Jesus into my life. He read through a little booklet with me called *The Four Spiritual Laws.* At the end he read the question "Is there any reason why you wouldn't want to invite Christ into your life at this time?"

Months before (though I didn't understand it at the time) my mother had invited Christ into her life at a Christian women's club. My sister, brother, and I had begun to attend church with her. As a result of the changes in her life, my father began to attend church with us. A short time later he, too, became a Christian. Even though I was young I could see positive changes in our home. So when my father talked to me in the hospital about Jesus, I was ready. There wasn't a reason in the world not to invite Christ into my life. I wanted to know Him.

So I know God. And I suspect that if you are reading this book, there is a good chance that you do, too. At some point in your life you invited Jesus into your heart. That is the first step. But to truly know God involves more.

Though I became a Christian at a young age, it took a crisis in my adult life to get my relationship with Christ to a place where I truly knew Him and could hear His voice and direction for my life. At the time I had become like the nation of Israel in Deuteronomy 8:11 TLB: "Beware that in your plenty you don't forget the Lord your God. . . ." When I speak about this subject, I find that many women are in the same place. They know God is out there. But life is going okay—they're in a time of plenty—and it's easy to forget God.

Most people say trauma brought them closer to God. It was certainly true in my life. For me, the death of my first business triggered the crisis. I know many people have faced far greater difficulties than I have, but our own problems always feel the worst. I remember crying out, "God, I thought this was where you wanted me!" I had been doing color analysis for eight years. I had written a book on it. I had traveled all over the country with my business. I could give you a long list of reasons why I was sure that was where God wanted me. Suddenly the phone quit ringing. No one wanted my expertise. I cried out to God constantly—to no avail. I didn't hear an answer.

Looking back, I realize I was not close enough to God to hear His voice. In John 10:14, 16 NCV Jesus tells us, "I am the good shepherd. I know my sheep, and my sheep know me. . . . They will listen to my voice." I had to get reacquainted with God.

If the Holy Spirit is touching your heart and telling you that you, too, need to get reacquainted with God, I encourage you to start now. Don't wait for a crisis. If you are experiencing a time of plenty, let this be your wake-up call to seek God's voice.

God used three tools to help me know Him again. The first was a particular Bible. Having grown up in the Christian community, I knew that I should read the Bible. From the example of others and the church's teaching, I believed I needed to read

through the Bible in a year. I tried many, many times—but always failed. My brain couldn't track the program that said I should read each day a little of the Old Testament, and some of the New Testament, Psalms, and Proverbs. I would make a check in each day's progress box, but I had no idea what I had read, so I did not stick with it. I bought a Bible that provided readings for each day of the year. I waited until January 1 and began in Genesis. I did okay through Genesis and Exodus but got bogged down in Leviticus. Before long I was so far behind I gave up—trying again the next year. I find that when I share this experience at speaking engagements, many women have had the same struggles and results.

Then I came across *The Narrated Bible* (published by Harvest House). It is unique in three ways that made a difference for me—and it may help you, as well. First, *The Narrated Bible* is arranged in chronological order; the text flows according to when events happened. I noticed the first real difference in Leviticus, the book of laws. In *The Narrated Bible*, Leviticus is interspersed into Genesis and Exodus. The laws are placed into the text with the events that spurred their creation. The laws took on new interest for me when they were a part of the story and not just a list of rules. Another area in which I experienced a deeper comprehension due to the chronological order was in the Psalms. Many Psalms are placed in with the books of Kings and Chronicles—among the battles or events that inspired the corresponding Psalm. The Psalms whose history are not known are arranged by topic. This chronological inclusion makes the text much more interesting, making it easier to stick with a Bible-reading program.

The second thing I found helpful about *The Narrated Bible* is that it is narrated. Descriptive commentary within the text offers cultural, historic, and geographic insights, tying the text together. While the narration increases understanding in many areas, two observations were especially interesting: I learned that Adam, the first man, was alive until the generation before Noah. I might have been able to do a timeline and figure this out, but I never would have. This bit of knowledge isn't life changing, but it's interesting to realize that Adam himself was around telling the story of Creation for many generations. Additionally, the narration opened my eyes to the life of Aaron and to God's forgiveness. I knew the story of Aaron and the golden calf; I can easily picture the drawings from my Sunday school books. I also knew that Aaron, Moses' brother, was made the high priest of Israel. However, until I read the narration, I did not realize that these "two Aarons" were one in the same. The narration said something like "If God could forgive Aaron for something as major as leading an entire nation away from God and then use him as the spiritual leader for that entire nation, couldn't God forgive you for anything you have done and use you? Have any of you done anything worse than leading an entire nation away from God?" Wow, what a concept! I would never have thought of that without the narration.

The third thing I found helpful about *The Narrated Bible* is that it is divided into 365 daily readings, but they are not dated! This meant I didn't have to wait until January to start, and when I got behind it wasn't so obvious, so I kept reading. I didn't finish the Bible in a year or read it every day, but I kept with it and understood what I read.

If you need to get to know God, *The Narrated Bible* might be as helpful for you as it was for me. Another tool that was instrumental in my life for getting reacquainted with God was a study of the names of God. I used to be almost irritated by the different names for God I'd encounter. I couldn't pronounce or understand half of them. When I came across what I considered a nickname for God (such as Adonai, El Roi, and Jehovah-Elohim), I would just substitute "God." As I learned more, however, I found that these names of God are far more than nicknames. They represent God's character, so by knowing the names of God, I know who God is. Two studies I suggest are the ones by Liz Curtis Higgs and Kay Arthur. Liz's is *Mirror, Mirror on the Wall, Have I Got News for You!* (published by Thomas Nelson), a light study that parallels how God views us and who God is. Kay's is a beautiful coffee table book called *To Know Him by Name* (published by Multnomah).

The third tool I recommend for your quest to know God is Oswald Chambers' devotional, *My Utmost for His Highest* (published by Discovery House). If, like me, you have tried this book before and struggled to comprehend it, I suggest that you try the updated edition in "today's language." With this new version, I became a fan of Chambers' work. Before, I had thought I wasn't very spiritual because I hadn't gained the same wisdom from the classic devotional as many of my older and saintly friends did. The updated edition showed me I was not unspiritual, just from a different generation.

Whether you use these tools that were helpful for me or others that work for you, to know God's purpose for your life requires that you first know *Him*.

Pray Without Ceasing

To know God we must also pray without ceasing. Paul says in 1 Thessalonians 5:17 NIV to "pray continually." In *The Living Bible* the verse is translated "always keep on praying." Numerous other places in the New Testament say virtually the same thing: "Pray at all times" (Romans 12:12 NCV); "Pray all the time" (Ephesians 6:18 TLB); and "Always pray" (Luke 18:1 NCV). Obviously, constant prayer is important. But as we read God's Word and study the life of Christ—our ultimate role model—we see that He did not pray always in the same sense we tend to think of prayer today. With so many books and seminars on prayer, I find that we have made prayer into a more formal activity than these verses and Christ's life suggest.

Christ was in constant prayer by His attitude of wanting His heavenly Father involved in everything He did. *The Life Application Study Bible* (published by Tyndale House) explains it this way:

We cannot spend all our time on our knees, but it is possible to have a prayerful attitude at all times. This attitude is built upon acknowledging our dependence on God, realizing his presence within us, and determining to obey him fully. Then we will find it natural to pray frequent, spontaneous, short prayers. A prayerful attitude is not a substitute for regular times of prayer but should be an outgrowth of those times.

In our daily lives this means that we should come to God all day long, both formally and informally, with the big and the little things in our lives. Most of us know to call on God for big concerns. Research indicates that 79 percent of Americans pray to God when they are at a crossroads in their lives.[1] For some reason, though, we feel like we shouldn't bother Him about little stuff.

Chuck and I had been married a year or so when he sold his car and bought his dream car—a 1963 E-Type Jaguar roadster. Unfortunately, if you plan to drive one of these cars every day, you need to work on it every night! Chuck would come home from work, change clothes, and disappear into the garage. Meanwhile, I would be cooking dinner. (I'm a gourmet cook with seventeen years of *Bon Appétit* in my kitchen right now. So when I say I'm cooking dinner, I'm really cooking dinner.) When dinner was ready, I'd holler out to the garage. Chuck would come in, eat, and head back out to his beloved Jaguar. As you might imagine, I grew tired of this quite quickly and didn't have the kindest thoughts about the car—or my husband.

One night, as I was grumbling to myself while doing the dishes, I decided to follow Christ's example in Matthew 14:23, where it says that He went up to the mountain to pray by himself. I went upstairs and into the bathroom, closed the door, and sat on the toilet. There I prayed that God would fix Chuck. While praying, I heard a virtually audible voice ask, "Who gives Chuck more pleasure, you or the car?" It may have been a perverse pleasure in my opinion, but I could see that with my nagging, the car was winning.

In the grand scheme of things, I had come to God with a silly little problem, but He cared enough to show me the answer. Chuck wasn't the problem. It was my attitude. And with God's help, I changed my perspective. Today I proudly display a plaque on my office wall for being the second-place navigator in the San Diego Jaguar Club! I keep the award as a reminder of God's power to change us when we let Him be a part of our entire life—even the little stuff.

In order to know and celebrate God's purpose for your life, pray continually. Have an attitude that includes God in every aspect of your life.

Ask

No matter our concerns, if we need help or direction on a specific issue, God's Word tells us to ask Him. My favorite verse on this subject is James 1:5, which *The Living Bible* presents with wonderful clarity: "If you want to know what God wants you to do, ask him, and he will gladly tell you, for he is always ready to give a bountiful supply of wisdom to all who ask him; he will not resent it." *The Life Application Study Bible* adds this insight to the Scripture: "By *wisdom*, James is talking not only about knowledge but about the ability to make wise decisions in difficult circumstances. Whenever we need wisdom, we can pray to God, and he will generously supply what we need. Christians don't have to grope around in the dark, hoping to stumble upon answers. We can ask for God's wisdom to guide our choices." Isn't that great? We don't have to grope around in the dark! We can allow God to guide our choices!

Other Scriptures echo the emphasis James 1:5 places on asking. Ezekiel 36:37 TLB tells us, "The Lord God says: 'I am ready to hear Israel's prayers for these blessings and to grant them their requests. Let them but ask. . . .'" James 4:2 NKJV continues, "You do not have because you do not ask." Clearly, asking for God's guidance is a part of the process.

I have spent many hours in prayer asking God to show me His purpose for my life. What is it that you are seeking direction for in your life right now? Whether it is big or small, ask Him.

"Because I am God's child, He is concerned about every aspect of my life. I like the three verbs in Luke 11:9 NIV: 'ASK and it will be given to you; SEEK and you will find; KNOCK and the door will be opened.'

"Ask, Seek and Knock are words of action for us. Even as much as we long to be rescued from problems, we still are responsible for the results. The Lord has promised to help us, to direct us, but we still have to take that first step in faith. And in Him, we can do exactly that!"

SANDRA P. ALDRICH,
SPEAKER AND AUTHOR

Wait

Waiting for God's direction is the part of the equation with which most of us have trouble. Let's face it, patience is not a part of our culture or upbringing. We're accustomed to instant everything, and we often expect God to work in the same way. Remember when you got your first microwave or your first computer? Weren't they amazing? Now I get impatient waiting for the microwave to boil water. My computer was top of the line when I bought it two years and three books ago. It was so much faster than the old one I passed on to my husband. Now he has rejected that one, too, in favor of one newer and faster than my current computer! Like the old ad for Hertz Rent-a-Car, we hate to wait!

But like it or not, God often wants us to wait. One of the many lessons we learn from the Old Testament is that waiting is how God operates sometimes. Moses was selected from childhood to save the Israelites, but he was thrown out of Egypt and spent forty years in a pasture with sheep before God called him into action. The nation of Israel waited for forty years to see the Promised Land. God could have done it differently. They could have taken a direct path, cleared by God. But God made the nation of Israel wait. Likewise, we usually have to wait when we are seeking God's purpose or His direction for our lives.

Many Old Testament verses tell us to wait on the Lord. Psalm 25:5 NKJV says, "On You I wait all the day." Psalm 27:14 TLB says, "Don't be impatient. Wait for the Lord. . . . Yes, wait and he will help you." I love Psalm 62:5 NKJV: "My soul, wait silently for God alone." I can just picture the psalmist reminding his soul to wait!

Looking back, the waiting I endured as my color analysis business died away was like being in a hallway. God had closed one door in my life, but I didn't want that door closed. I didn't want to end my business—it was all I knew. To prevent it from closing, I kept a couple of fingers between the doorjamb and the door.

I was afraid to take a "real" job. What if someone called and wanted their colors done? I worked five flexible jobs to make ends meet yet be available should someone need my services. No one did. As long as I held on to my past, I was unable to move down the hallway to the door God had waiting for me. By keeping my fingers in the doorway, I was held in that dark place, crying to God rather than reaching out for the new plan He had for my life.

I believe that while we wait for God's answer, perhaps even impatiently, He wants us to keep doing the best we can. We shouldn't give up on life and lie down, waiting for a lightning bolt to guide us. Again we look to the Old Testament for evidence of God's provision.

Abraham was seventy-five when God told him he would become a father, and he was one hundred when Isaac was born (Genesis 12:4; 21:5). Abraham waited twenty-five years for God's promise to be fulfilled. Moses spent forty years in the desert before fulfilling God's call on his life. Both Abraham and Moses continued their duties during this time of waiting. For me, that meant continuing to work in some way or another.

Now I can see how God used that time to give me additional skills and to prepare me for His future plans. One job I had during this time of waiting—in the hallway of my life— was as a lecturer for the Fashion Institute of Design and Merchandising in Los Angeles. I went to high schools throughout the region and spoke about careers in the industry. I had to memorize prepared speeches on a number of topics. For history classes, I talked about fashionable first ladies. In art classes, I discussed the elements of design. And for math classes, I addressed the importance of numbers and measurements. While this job wasn't one of my favorites (kids often viewed my presence as an opportunity to sleep, write notes, or catch up on homework), it was great training for my current place in life as a speaker and trainer of speakers.

During this time I also worked for a Christian greeting card company. After my lectures I'd visit Christian bookstores in the area and sell them greeting cards. Unfortunately, once I got the cards into the stores, they didn't sell well. Still, being in bookstores gave me a wonderful education of the industry.

"Why would a woman blessed with all the spiritual opportunities of this time in history settle for doing what comes naturally when she can learn to do what is God's purpose?"

GAYLE ROPER,
SPEAKER AND AUTHOR

I can say with confidence (and thanks) that lecturing to high school students and selling greeting cards—done during my "waiting" time—were not God's long-term plan for my life. Yet God used both jobs as an invaluable education that has added to my life today. How many speakers have that kind of challenging training ground and how many authors have that kind of understanding of the people who sell books?

So we wait. Waiting for God's direction and purpose in our lives, His answer to our requests for guidance.

Weigh Your Thoughts

When we know God, have an attitude that involves Him in every aspect of our lives, ask for specific direction, and wait for the answer, we can trust that eventually His answer will come. Sometimes it will come through Scripture. Even if we've read a passage before, God will cause an insight to jump off the page like a red flag. The answer may come through circumstances that are beyond coincidence. It may be found through the wise counsel of godly friends, or we may hear God's voice loud and clear in our head.

I have sensed God's direction in each of these forms. However the answer comes, it is important that we weigh our thoughts to be sure they are truly God's plan for us and not our own. Sometimes we want something so badly and wait so long that we misread circumstances or the little voice in our head.

Many years ago at a CLASSeminar, a woman believed that while she was there God had given her direction for her life. This isn't a goal of our program but it does happen frequently. Taking three days out of your daily routine to learn new skills that God can use seems to bring purpose and direction to many people. So when this woman told the teaching team that she had received God's direction, we eagerly waited to hear what she had to say. She announced that she was going to go home, divorce her husband, and go into full-time speaking. Needless to say, we were shocked.

In cases like this, we need to weigh our thoughts against God's Word. Yes, divorce does happen. Sometimes it is the only option. But it is never God's perfect plan for our lives. Without certain aspects of a relationship in place, God is not going to advise someone to go home and divorce her husband. Though this woman was sure that she had heard God's voice, weighing her thoughts against a basic knowledge of Scripture, it's clear to see that this was her own subconscious mind advising her, not God.

So first weigh your thoughts against God's Word.

Sometimes the answer you perceive is not so clearly addressed in Scripture. At these times you need to seek godly counsel from Christian friends whose lives exhibit the fruit of the Spirit, or from your pastor, his wife, or a Bible study leader. Tell them your prayers and the answer you perceive. Ask them to pray with you to help you determine if this truly is of God.

In my case, I had been praying for three years asking for God's direction for my life. During that time I had become reacquainted with God and was getting close to Him so I could "hear His voice." I had finally let go of my color analysis business and the door that He had closed in my life.

I remember where I was when I heard God's voice loud and

clear. I was driving between San Bernardino, where my parents' office was at the time, and San Diego, where Chuck and I lived at the time. I had been praying, which I often did on that two-hour trek, and was focused on God and His purpose for my life. Suddenly God clearly laid out for me a ten-year plan. I finally had the answer I had been seeking. I got home that night, eager to tell Chuck everything, but I couldn't find the words to express what I felt God had told me.

Several days later I was able to explain the guidance I had received. God had clearly shown me that in ten years my business or ministry would be a central clearinghouse for Christian communicators. Since there was nothing like this at the time, I was unclear about what it all meant or how I would be involved, but I was confident that this direction was from God. It certainly did not conflict with any biblical principle, but I still needed to weigh my thoughts.

First, I talked to my husband, who agreed with and

> "One step ahead is all I now can see,
> But He who notes the sparrow's fall, He leadeth me.
> Not only by the waters still my feet may tread,
> But with my hand in His, I know that I am led.
> And for the lonely, rocky way, whate'er the length,
> He has shod my feet with patience and with strength.
> So, though the pathway smooth or rough may be,
> Oh, joyful thought, my Father leadeth me!"
>
> ELLA B. DOXSEE

supported the idea. Next, I would talk with my parents, who were returning in a few days from their first ministry trip to Australia. After picking them up at the airport and stopping at a gas station, I told my mother about hearing God's direction. She began to cry, then said, "Your father and I have been praying that you would work with us in the ministry. But we didn't want to ask you because we wanted it to be your idea." That was the confirmation I needed. The next day I quit all my jobs and began to develop a central clearinghouse for Christian communicators. I didn't know exactly what that entailed or where it would lead me, but as God opened doors, I walked through them.

Since that day on the highway it's been exciting to see how completely God has fulfilled the purpose He gave me. One of the first things I developed was a speakers' service. Churches from all over the country called our office to invite my mother to speak for them. If she wasn't available, I'd offer the services of a teaching team from our CLASSeminar, which ultimately led to the pool of the more than 150 Christian speakers we have available today. I developed resources to help train people to be more effective communicators and meeting planners. Later I created the CLASS Reunion, a networking event designed to connect speakers who want to write books with publishers who need authors.

After doing this as part of my parents' ministry for nine years, they announced they were ready to step out of the day-to-day operations of the entity I had created. We agreed to a four-year plan under which I would take over. Three months later, however, my father announced out of the blue that they saw no reason to wait four years. Rather, they wanted the transition completed by the end of the year.

I was thrown out of my comfort zone and again searched for God's direction. As I prayed about the situation, I realized that it had been exactly ten years from the time God had given me the original vision for CLASS! I had to seek God's will. Was it time to move on to something else, or did this mean I should take CLASS over and make it truly mine?

"If you think God is speaking to you,
Weigh your thoughts against His Word.
If there's any contradiction,
It's not His voice you've heard.
For God will never direct you
To do something contrary to His will,
And you'll never receive such instruction
In His voice so small and still."

LEONA LAKE RYAN

Well, you know by now that I did agree to take over the ownership and management of the various services I had created. I had again sought advice and made the decision that this was what I was supposed to do. Isaiah 55:8 NIV says, "'For my thoughts are not your thoughts, neither are your ways my ways,' declares the Lord." Be sure that as you seek direction you weigh your thoughts to confirm that they are God's thoughts and not simply your wanting something so badly that you assume your thoughts are God's thoughts.

Because I feel confident of God's purpose for my life, I have a support system that carries me through difficult times: when

> *"And I said to the man who stood at the gate of the year, 'Give me a light that I may tread safely into the unknown.' And he replied, 'Go out into the darkness and put your hand into the hand of God. That shall be to you better than light and safer than a known way.'"*
>
> LOUISE HASKINS,
> EDUCATOR AND WRITER

bills far outweigh income, when employee problems get me down, and when seminar registrations don't meet expectations. Sometimes I get discouraged. I think again about selling real estate. But then I seek God's direction, and usually through circumstances that are far beyond coincidence, God shows me that I still belong here. Even the fact that you are reading this book is an affirmation to me.

As you seek God's purpose for your life, first be sure you truly know God. If this requires spending some time getting reacquainted with Him, take the necessary steps to do so. Whether you use the tools I suggested earlier in this chapter or something else you find on your own, be sure you know Him. Then develop an attitude that involves God in every aspect of your life, even the little things. Ask Him for specific guidance and wait for the answer. When the answer comes, whatever form it takes, weigh your thoughts first against Scripture and then with godly counsel. Don't act until you have the assurance that what you are planning is of God.

It is also important to realize that God may want you somewhere else tomorrow. When God closes a door in your life, let go. Move down the hallway to the next door He has opened for you. My personal experience with God, and what I have read in the Old Testament, tell me that while the unknown can be scary, what God has for us on the other side of the door is always greater, bigger, or brighter.

Thank Him

Once we have a sense of divine purpose, Scripture tells us that we must thank God. Philippians 4:6 TLB wraps this up perfectly: "Don't worry about anything; instead, pray about everything; tell God your needs, and don't forget to thank him for his answers." When you do this, you will have the complete confidence of knowing that you are where God wants you!

"Lord, teach me to listen. The times are noisy and my ears are weary with the thousand raucous sounds which continuously assault them. Give me the spirit of the boy Samuel when he said to Thee, 'Speak, for thy servant heareth.'

"Let me hear Thee speaking in my heart. Let me get used to the sounds of Thy Voice, that its tones may be familiar when the sounds of the earth die away and the only sound will be the music of Thy speaking Voice. Amen." [2]

— A. W. TOZER

Celebrate Your Personality

Finding Balance in Who God Made You to Be

Chapter 4

If Mary Todd Lincoln were First Lady today, she might well be applauded—or at least accepted. Instead, as mentioned earlier, some say her outspokenness and eccentricities landed her in a private sanitarium for four months in 1875 (though the true state of her mental health is still debated). In any case, it's clear that those of us who do not fit the stereotypical image of a "lady" are not shunned as much as we might have been in the past. Indeed, our strong personalities are often rewarded. This honor seems to depend on whether a woman has learned to rein in any extreme personality traits. Perhaps if Mrs. Lincoln had worked on being more balanced she might have received more respect.

Finding balance in our personality is an important area of self-improvement. Women who are extremely loud, bold, or brassy are still criticized today. Those on the other end of the spectrum—mousy, shy, and introverted—are also looked down upon.

Twenty years ago I did a presentation for my Toastmasters' club. On two display boards I compared headlines from the covers of popular women's and men's magazines. In short, women were reading about personal and spiritual growth, men were not. My point to men: They'd better get their act together or women would surpass them. We were growing and they were not.

It's interesting to see how far women have come in two decades. All that personal growth must have paid off. Whether it is our genes or our culture, women tend to embrace change and growth. It's not always easy, though.

Good Morning America recently did a feature on Hillary Rodham Clinton.[1] They profiled her public life beginning with Bill's first run for office, Arkansas state attorney general. At the time, Hillary took a stand of individuality and refused to give in to pressure to become fashionable. She kept her maiden name and worked in her law practice. When Bill lost the next election, she remade herself into a more "acceptable" wife. The TV segment chronicled how Hillary had repeatedly been strong and assertive only to be criticized for it. She'd tone down her image into a more acceptable political partner, then have her strong personality resurface and face criticism again. This cycle has repeated over and over in her life. Somehow she has failed to learn to temper her personality.

Compare Hillary to another very public and very forceful woman, Elizabeth Dole. "Liddy" is considered a trailblazer with equally strong characteristics. "There's no question she's smart, charming and one of the best speakers on the national stage," says Ann Blackman, Washington, D.C., *Time* correspondent. "But she is so controlling that everything she does has to be carefully programmed."[2] Though controlling, Elizabeth has learned to make the most of her strengths—smart and charming—while minimizing her weaknesses. She has found balance, just as each of us needs to do.

Perhaps the reason the feminist movement has declined is that the women we picture as feminists are those who exhibit extreme behaviors. Women who are loud, insist on getting their way, and try to take over do not represent the average woman today. They are the extreme. In 1998 only 32 percent of women surveyed had a favorable view of feminists, down from 44 percent in 1989.[3]

Girls and young women can get away with personality traits on the outermost end of the scale. However, as we mature, the very things that once seemed attractive can easily alienate others. Have you ever heard someone comment on the behavior of another, saying something like "It might have worked as a child, but she's too old to get away with it now!"? The cute, young cheerleader who is leader of her clique, always gets her way, and has a quick retort to criticism is viewed as sassy and smart. Imagine those same traits in a forty- or fifty-year-old woman in the workplace or on a church committee. She's bossy, brassy, and obnoxious. The high school student who is always on time, sits quietly in class, and does not attract attention to herself is viewed as organized and demure, perhaps even coy. Take those traits into the adult world and that same person is sometimes viewed as boring, dull, and maybe rigid. Either scenario opens us up for criticism because they represent extremes and make us appear uncontrolled, lacking balance.

As Christian women with the ultimate goal of becoming more like Christ, celebrating our personality means allowing the Holy Spirit to minimize our weak traits and strengthen us in other areas in order to become more balanced, more perfect, and more like Christ!

> "Just as an artist paints upon a canvas using a chosen palette of colors, so do human beings build a life combining unique sets of colors that define who we are."
>
> CAROLYN WARNER,
> EDUCATIONAL AND
> POLITICAL LEADER

The Personalities

I learned about personality traits thirty years ago from my mother, an expert on personalities, and I have been teaching the subject for twenty years.

When I speak about personalities, I always start by asking my audience, "How many of you have noticed there are people out there who are different from you?" With laughter, virtually everyone raises their hand.

Recognizing these differences is nothing new. More than two thousand years ago the great Greek philosopher Hippocrates observed that some people were loud, fun-loving, and undisciplined. Others were neat, organized, and tended to see the negatives of life. Many people were born leaders who were goal-oriented but bossy. Still others were easygoing and friendly but lacked self-motivation.

Being a physician, Hippocrates studied these various people to figure out what made them different. With the limited scientific knowledge available in his day, he concluded each type of person had a specific fluid in his or her body. Despite this primitive premise, the fluids' Greek names have been used over the centuries to describe these personality types: Sanguine, Melancholy, Choleric, and Phlegmatic.

To bring ancient thought up to date (and because the Greek words are hard to pronounce), we add the modern adjectives Popular, Perfect, Powerful, and Peaceful to the original, time-tested Greek terms, so you have the Popular Sanguine, Perfect Melancholy, Powerful Choleric, and Peaceful Phlegmatic. These terms, known collectively as the "Personalities," are not labels but rather a vocabulary by which we discuss our own set of strengths and weakness.

To help you determine your personality type, work through the Personality Profile in the Appendix. If you are familiar with the Personalities already, please continue reading this chapter since the applications here are fresh and new. (For more information on this subject, read *Personality Plus* by Florence Littauer, *Personality Puzzle* and *Getting Along With Almost Anybody*, both by Florence and Marita Littauer, and *A Woman's Guide to the Temperaments* by Donna Partow. All are available through your local bookstore or by calling CLASS at 800/433-6633.)

No one is 100 percent one personality type. We are all unique individuals. However, most of us do function within a main or primary personality type with an equally strong or weaker secondary personality. Usually each of us has a smattering of traits from all the personality categories but our primary and secondary personality traits are strongest.

One of the things I find most valuable about the Personalities is that they give us a benchmark for measuring

> *"Accepting my strengths and recognizing my weaknesses sets me free to use the unique gifts God has given me to follow the passions and dreams He has planted within me."*
>
> BETTY SOUTHARD,
> SPEAKER AND WRITER

personal growth. When we understand our personality, we see a list of strengths and weaknesses that are attributed to our particular personality. As women comfortable with the idea of growth, we can use this information to improve ourselves and become more balanced.

Knowing your personality is the first step toward growing within the person God made you to be. Understanding your strengths, working to minimize your weaknesses, and learning skills that are not natural to you will make you more balanced.

The Popular Sanguine

The bumper sticker "Are we having fun yet?" aptly summarizes the motto of the Popular Sanguine. This woman is a natural optimist. She's a "talker" who enjoys people because they provide an audience for her never-ending stories. The Popular Sanguine is usually considered funny even though she is not a joke teller. Unusual things happen to the Popular Sanguine, and her recounting of the episode keeps everyone laughing. She also thrives on attention, which may explain her attraction to unique, artsy, and trendy clothes. She wants everyone to be happy and everyone to love her. These desires combine to make the Popular Sanguine the natural codependent of life, working hard to cheer others up, even changing who she is if it will help. Relationships are very important to the Popular Sanguine.

CHARMING

Most Popular Sanguines are naturally charming. Charm is a wonderful strength. As a child, someone with charm is thought of as being delightful and even cute. However, in later years, without the balance of maturity, this same trait can become irresponsible and immature. Popular Sanguines may be tempted to charm their way out of trouble. I should know; I was frequently stopped for speeding when I was young. But I'd bat my eyelashes, flirt with the officer, and seldom get a ticket. I knew it was time for me to be more responsible and pay attention to my driving when I got pulled over and my best tactics had no impact. I got the ticket. The wiles of my youth were no longer effective.

Like me, Gail DiMarco is a Popular Sanguine who is learning to find balance in her life. She says,

> *"You find yourself refreshed by the presence of cheerful people. Why not make an honest effort to confer that pleasure on others? Half the battle is gained if you never allow yourself to say anything gloomy."*
>
> LYDIA CHILD, ABOLITIONIST, NOVELIST, AND EDITOR

When I was old enough to realize I was charming, I began to use charm as a way of getting what I wanted: jobs, boyfriends, leadership positions, selling my ideas to others. I learned to turn on the charm—a sure thing for a Popular Sanguine to get what she wants.

At the age of forty-five this same charm still works very well. However, charm somehow overshadowed my intelligence, and I do not think this is a good thing for me personally. Why? Because I would like to be known more for my knowledge, for people to seek my advice, to respect me for what I can bring to the table, not just charm. I am very thankful for the way God has created me. And I do like myself, even my charm. However, I feel I have been missing something. Charm is not enough for me anymore. I know it works with others. But now I need to raise the bar for myself. Just once I would love for someone to say, "Gail DiMarco is so bright."

TALKATIVE STORYTELLER

Besides their charm, Popular Sanguines are known for being talkative and great storytellers. At their best, they are entertaining and the life of the party. However, unchecked, this trait can easily cause a person to exaggerate or to monopolize a conversation.

I was at a party recently with many people I hadn't seen for years. Everyone was having a great time catching up on each other's lives. Clusters of conversation could be seen throughout the room when Sandy blew in—late. It had been years since we had seen her, but we all knew that Sandy was very funny and entertaining. Unfortunately, her personality had not tempered. She burst into a conversation in which I was involved and began her own hilarious dialogue—monopolizing everyone's attention. If you are a Popular Sanguine, be careful not to interrupt others. Learn to listen more and talk less.

Sharon now calls herself a "Satisfied Sanguine," but it wasn't always that way:

Sometimes I think that the moment I came from my mother's womb I entertained the doctors and nurses and thought I was supposed to entertain everyone. I distinctly remember singing my first solo in church at the age of four and from that moment on I craved attention and applause.

My mother and father divorced when I was five, and mother had to take a job in beer joints or night-clubs, since she lacked education. That was no prob-lem for me because they allowed her to bring me with her and I always sang for the customers. Once, when she worked in a nightclub, the orchestra leader let me sing while they were practicing. Everywhere I went I was asked to sing. Once, while singing where mother worked, a man heard me and asked mother's permis-sion to let me audition for a live radio program. She gave him permission and I soon became a regular on that radio station. They called me "Little Sherry Lee." I had an uncle who was a preacher. He often let me sing at his church and that was where I really enjoyed myself.

While a baby Christian, God opened many doors

for me to share my testimony and sing. About fifteen years into my walk with Him the singing stopped. I became depressed and suicidal. Yet, once He had my attention He let me know that He was restructuring my life. With the power of the Holy Spirit He altered my personality.

It has taken God several years to teach me that my self-worth shouldn't be centered on my ability to sing, but rather on who He created me to be. As He taught me to walk by faith and not by sight, I found that there were other positive aspects and gifts that He wanted to use, and some calming down I had to do. Now I enjoy working one-on-one with a hurting person as much as I love speaking or singing in front of thousands. He is recreating me but leaving me with the same personality. I no longer crave to be the center of attention. Now He opens doors for it to happen. I am now a Satisfied Sanguine.

QUICK-WITTED

With a fast response to everything, the Popular Sanguine is known for her quick wit. This trait is encouraged in childhood and applauded by adults. At family gatherings, young Popular Sanguines often entertain with their unplanned, snappy retorts to others' comments. They're affectionately called sassy. With this instigation, it's easy to see why so many Popular Sanguine women grow up to be brassy, obnoxious, and loud. As a Popular Sanguine, it is difficult to recognize when sassy becomes brassy. We might overhear people refer to our quick wit in a derogatory way, which is troubling because the trait used to garner praise.

With the power of the Holy Spirit, however, we Popular Sanguines can aim for quiet dignity. We can tone down our volume of speech and laughter. It may help to ask your husband or a close friend to point out Popular Sanguines who display offensive traits. Seeing how foolish a person appears to others—walking into a room speaking loudly and waving their arms with enthusiasm—has helped me to tone down my approach. I've learned to be quiet and not enter a conversation unless I'm invited or asked a question. It's tough. I recently told my husband, "I bet your friends think I'm really boring." We Popular Sanguines may not see it ourselves, but when we are striving to show quiet dignity, others still feel our energy and excitement. My husband assured me no one thought I was boring. Whew!

LaMarilys Doering was very much the sassy Sanguine in school. She reported,

> I wanted to be in the middle of everything and usually was. As an adult, I have had to learn some self-control. I can be the life of the party, but I also love to turn the spotlight on others and step back. Now I am a reserved Sanguine. I can now wait in anticipation of learning something more. I'm a frustrated teacher and I've found I cannot teach without learning.

As we Popular Sanguines work to bring balance and maturity into our personality, a good verse for us to take to heart is 1 Peter 3:4 TLB: "Be beautiful inside, in your hearts, with the lasting charm of a gentle and quiet spirit." Because that quiet and gentle spirit is not something that comes naturally to us, it is something we have to work on, something we have to learn. But with the Holy Spirit's power, it is something we can achieve!

The Powerful Choleric

Like the Nike commercials, the motto for the Powerful Choleric is "Just do it." The Powerful Choleric is the doer or worker of life. She gains self-worth from accomplishment and has a mental checklist in her head. Before going to sleep, she reviews her day's accomplishments. If she's accomplished more than anyone else she knows, she'll sleep well. If not, she's been known to get up and do more! The Powerful Choleric is a natural leader, often taking over the household in her childhood. She learns early on that she is usually right. This combination makes her quickly rise to the top of groups or organizations. Unfortunately, her personality isn't conducive to developing friendships; friends seem to get in the way of "doing."

Many traits of a Powerful Choleric receive attention and are admired in today's society. Likewise, the weaknesses and flaws are also quite noticeable. For this reason, it is especially important for the Powerful Choleric woman to learn to temper her personality. Strength in women has been accepted only recently, and those who haven't learned to temper their personality—and come off as overbearing—are open for judgment.

> "I am extraordinarily patient provided I get my own way in the end."
>
> MARGARET THATCHER, FORMER BRITISH PRIME MINISTER

Golden, a Powerful Choleric married to a pastor, told me she and her husband became very frustrated at people's reactions when they ministered together. "Various acquaintances and friends report being intimidated and threatened by me, when that has never been my intention." When Golden voiced an opinion regarding church administrative matters, an elder was unhappy and made her feel that God was unhappy with her, too. Through much time and prayer, she learned the Lord was pleased with her. "He began to show me that the qualities I have are exactly what He wanted in me to accomplish the purpose for which He designed me. I simply need to be more sensitive to other personalities . . . and, as a woman in ministry, especially in dealing with men." Powerful Choleric women like Golden need to learn to be more sensitive.

RIGHT

Like Popular Sanguines, Powerful Cholerics are quick thinkers. Couple that with their unique ability to correctly assess a situation, and it's not surprising that Powerful Cholerics learn early on that they're usually right. As you can imagine, though, being right is not always popular. As a child, the Powerful Choleric is considered bright and knowledgeable. But left unchecked, these traits can produce a know-it-all woman. To celebrate your Powerful Choleric personality, some adjustments are needed. First, realize that others may be right, too. There often is more than one right way to accomplish a task or reach a goal. Job 6:25 NKJV says, "How forceful are right words! But what does your arguing prove?" Additionally, as a Powerful Choleric, resist offering advice unless requested.

Cheyenne Bradford, a Powerful Choleric, says,

All my life, even as a young child, I felt that I always knew the answer, and that "my" way was the best way. I felt that other people would mess things up, so I would usually wind up doing things myself because I wanted them done "right." Even now, at forty-four (and I should know better), it's hard for me to "let go" and accept help from others. I always thought that if I accepted help, it was a sign of weakness—but God is working with me in that area. I usually think that if I give myself enough time to think about a situation, I'll eventually come up with the right solution.

Like Cheyenne, let God work with you; let others help you.

NATURAL LEADER

One of the trademarks of Powerful Cholerics is their

inborn tendency toward leadership positions. Any time there is a leadership vacuum, the Powerful Choleric steps in without hesitation. If there is a leader who is not doing a good job (or the Powerful Choleric perceives she is not), the leadership may fall to the Powerful Choleric—officially or unofficially. In school these qualities are praised. The Powerful Choleric frequently is the room monitor or class president. Undisciplined, these character qualities can result in being pushy and overbearing as an adult. As you celebrate your personality, resist pushing others to do things your way or to accept your program. Lead but don't push; request but don't order. A Powerful Choleric woman who is too bossy can easily intimidate and offend others.

One woman told me about her Powerful Choleric friend who discovered that the things she'd considered attributes had gotten out of control when her son married a Powerful Choleric with different views than her own!

Admired as a child for being resourceful and capable, my friend Clare developed into a woman who used her natural leadership abilities to take friends on cross-country tent camping trips. She trimmed trees, did carpentry, served as a hospice nurse, and is a garage sale addict. Early in her married life when funds were tight, she took it as her challenge to furnish her house and provide most needs, other than food, from the rummage of others—hence her love of garage sales.

Having grown accustomed to her methods, her

husband, children, nieces, and nephews delighted in the "finds" she made and gave to them. They looked forward to the second-hand Christmas variety, knowing they would have more because she could get it for less. Their interest fueled her search. One of Clare's greatest pleasures was finding a unique item that especially fit a gift recipient.

When her son married, she found that her daughter-in-law didn't share the enthusiasm that her own children had developed for her take-charge attitude. Clare's daughter-in-law was aghast at the thought of receiving a second-hand gift. She was appalled that Clare would invade her house for a week, even willing to sleep on the garage floor if there was no room in the house (it reminded Clare of camping), and refinish and re-hang all the doors in the house. Clare couldn't understand why her new daughter-in-law didn't view her helpful behavior positively. Clare sputtered, "All my life I've made-do creatively, been resourceful, capable of taking care of myself and others as well as being independent." But her daughter-in-law didn't "think it seemly." The trait that seemed to get her places and to which her family had adapted didn't fit with an adult coming into the family with another viewpoint. Her daughter-in-law felt that Clare was pushy and overbearing.

Ephesians 4:2 NCV offers a great reminder to Powerful

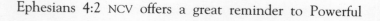

Choleric women who want more balance in their personality type: "Always be humble, gentle, and patient, accepting each other in love." Make it a personal goal to be humble, gentle, and patient. Prayerfully ask the Holy Spirit to help you accept others, even when their viewpoint is different from yours. With a bit of effort, the Powerful Choleric can bring her personality into balance so she is not constantly fighting to keep her strong nature hidden. She can be strong and in control yet still be humble and gentle.

The Perfect Melancholy

You've heard it before, perhaps you've even said it, "If it is worth doing, it is worth doing right." For the Perfect Melancholy, this maxim is a way of life. She tries hard to be perfect and assumes everyone else wants to be the same way. Sometimes her own standards of perfection are unattainable, even by her own doing. This lack of perfection or sense of failure can plunge her into depression.

The Perfect Melancholy avoids attracting attention to herself and, unlike the Popular Sanguine, buys traditional style clothing and appreciates basic selections of enduring value. She is scheduled, organized, and detail-conscious, keeping calendars and lists to make sure she does things on time and correctly. Many people see the Perfect Melancholy as the "thinker" of life. She is orderly; even the things no one sees, like her closets and drawers, are neat and clean. While the Perfect Melancholy is a caring and sensitive person, she tends

> *"Striving for excellence motivates you; striving for perfection is demoralizing."*
>
> HARRIET BRAIKER,
> PSYCHOLOGIST

to be suspicious of people and makes friends cautiously, often having one or two "best friends" who last a lifetime.

If you find yourself predominantly in the Perfect Melancholy category, be careful that the very things once worn as a badge of honor have not become a controlling force that is hurting your life and relationships today.

ORGANIZED

One of the first characteristics we think of for the Perfect Melancholy woman is her excellent organizational skills. Those of us with other personalities long for her natural affinity for planning and structure. If you are the parent or teacher of a Perfect Melancholy child, you know how wonderful this ability is. They are very tidy. They keep their room clean without needing to be constantly prodded. Their toys are in order. The Perfect Melancholy child is the natural student, writing down assignments and being in her seat on time. While this is certainly an admirable quality, it can go too far. Life is seldom perfect. The Perfect Melancholy must learn to be flexible since the best-laid plans can go awry.

Without growing and seeking balance in her life, the Perfect Melancholy can easily become rigid, making life harder for everyone—especially herself. To ensure this does not happen to you, develop an acceptance of others' imperfections. In our household, my Perfect Melancholy husband has adopted the sayings "Not everything worth doing is worth doing right" and "Sometimes good enough is good enough." Another growth step for the Perfect Melancholy is to lighten up on your schedule. Don't allow it to keep you from seeing and meeting others' needs.

Patty Lauterjung had to let go of some of her organized, perfectionistic tendencies as a result of a recent computer crash she experienced. As a Perfect Melancholy she had been a very organized and tidy child. "My room was very neat and my closet was organized. My first car as a teenager was spotless inside and out—subsequent cars have been very clean, too." Patty told me that she had been working on materials for a seminar she and her husband, Paul, were to be teaching in two weeks. The computer needed some work, and a Popular Sanguine friend from church offered to fix the problem. In the process, all the computer files, including their script, were lost. Patty continues the story:

This put my organized, tidy personality into orbit. There was much prayer going on with me as I knew how my personality would handle it at first. My actual comments included: This should have never happened!! Thank goodness I have hard copies!! Why didn't he check the backup to be sure it worked!! This is frustrating!! I had no control over this!! It wouldn't have happened with me!! Don't plan to go anywhere, Paul, until we get this fixed!! We need to clean up this office!!

It took over fifteen hours to recreate or scan hard copies and edit our script and masters because I wanted them looking "perfect" and the scanner had made errors. I'm still working on the script! My Popular Sanguine husband Paul is sleeping like a baby all night while I toss and turn.

I feel a bit more relaxed now, especially when I trust God and not myself to get things done. Otherwise I get overwhelmed at all there is to do and can't get started working. This whole experience is teaching me an area in my personality that God still needs to have control over—perfection.

SENSITIVE

Being sensitive and caring often makes the Perfect Melancholy woman a valued friend. I have a Perfect Melancholy friend, and she is the one I call when I need a listening ear or a shoulder to cry on. She doesn't try to give me answers right away or try to fix me. What special qualities in a friend. Still, these strengths can become a weakness if unchecked. Many Perfect Melancholies become hypersensitive, even temperamental. This same friend of mine has had to work at not taking everything so personally that she gets hurt and moody.

Being with someone who is hypersensitive is like walking on eggshells. If you aren't careful, there will be problems. As a Perfect Melancholy, take care that your sensitive spirit does not become the problem. Learn to look for the positives in life to cheer you up.

Speaker and author Kathy Collard Miller is a Perfect Melancholy who has had to work on this area in her life. She told me this story:

My Perfect Melancholy characteristic of being sensitive escalated in my adult years when I got married. Larry and I seemed matched for each other, yet shortly after the honeymoon was over, I felt hurt when his Powerful Choleric nature tried to tell me how to stack the glasses in the kitchen cupboard. (I didn't know about the Personalities then, so I thought he had started hating me.) Then as time went along, my hurt from being super-sensitive turned into anger toward him when his main goal in life wasn't to make me happy and meet my needs. I had become hypersensitive, offended by any little thing he did that to me indicated he didn't love me anymore. When that was added to my low self-esteem, I knew he secretly wanted to divorce me after just seven years of marriage.

God was faithful in healing our marriage and now we've been married almost twenty-nine years. We've even written a book together called *When the Honeymoon's Over*. I can see now that my sensitivity got me in trouble because I interpreted many of his actions and comments to mean "He doesn't love me anymore." As I have grown, matured, and become more balanced, I am secure in his love. He can give me his strong opinion in a Powerful Choleric way and I do not take it personally, but instead understand how he thinks. Because of the power of the Holy Spirit in me, I am grateful that I have mellowed to the point that I am no longer hypersensitive.

Rigidity and hypersensitivity are symptoms of selfishness: looking toward your own needs before the needs of others. To help bring balance and maturity into your life as a Perfect Melancholy, memorize Philippians 2:3–4 NCV, "When you do things, do not let selfishness or pride be your guide. Instead, be humble and give more honor to others than to yourselves. Do not be interested only in your own life, but be interested in the lives of others." By keeping your eyes on others and their needs, you will find that your own schedule becomes less important—allowing more flexibility into your life—and you will be less concerned by what people say about you.

Peaceful Phlegmatic

The Peaceful Phlegmatic is the opposite of the highly opinionated Powerful Choleric. Peaceful Phlegmatics go with the flow and let others worry over the details. Common lines you'll hear from the Peaceful Phlegmatic are "I don't care, it doesn't matter. Whatever is easiest." In fact, few things warrant getting, as my Peaceful Phlegmatic grandmother used to say, all "geehawed" up about. The Peaceful Phlegmatic is the most content of all the Personalities. She enjoys the status quo, is quiet, listens well, and is easy to get along with. While the Peaceful Phlegmatic likes people and has many friends, she especially enjoys watching people—hence her reputation as the "watcher" of life.

Since the Peaceful Phlegmatic is the most naturally quiet and gracious personality type, her weaknesses—areas that need growth—are less obvious. Still, even the Peaceful Phlegmatic needs some balance, especially in our modern society. Unlike the Powerful Choleric who needs to tone down her style, the Peaceful Phlegmatic needs to learn to speak up and get involved to truly celebrate her personality.

QUIET

Everyone appreciates a person who has a quiet and gracious spirit. Depending on the Bible version, the words "be quiet" are found ten to thirty times in Scripture. Surely quietness is a quality God encourages, and the Peaceful Phlegmatic already has it! While being quiet is admirable, the Peaceful Phlegmatic needs to be careful that the attribute others think is coy in childhood does not come off in adulthood as being detached. Because the Peaceful Phlegmatic woman prefers to stay in the background, it is easy for her to become so removed that she avoids life and taking risks if she does not make a conscious effort to grow and mature in this area. If you are a Peaceful Phlegmatic, learn to speak up and offer an opinion when you have one. Ask the Holy Spirit to give you strength when you feel weak or afraid.

Elaine Hardt is a Peaceful Phlegmatic who has learned to

> *"It is not that I lack ambition. I am ambitious in the sense that I want to be more than I am now. But if I were truly ambitious, I think I'd already be more than I am now."*
>
> JANE WAGNER,
> HUMORIST AND WRITER

speak up and take risks. She says,

I'm a quiet, thoughtful person. As a child I was appreciated by my parents and by my teachers. I didn't get into mischief, I was motivated to do well and study hard. Though I was quiet, I gradually learned I had a right to an opinion and I'd better state it. I saw people around me who could tease, joke around, give their opinions, and they were fun to be around.

I have learned to pray: not the *que sera, sera* type; not the passive "blessing" prayer; but to agree with God's Word and stand against the Enemy with determination. I have seen people healed, lives changed, wonderful things happen because this is what God wants to do. Faith is not passive. Faith says to God, "Teach me, show me, I am available." As I have learned to speak up and step out, I have written twelve books and had nearly two hundred articles published in seventy-seven different publications. Life is exciting because God takes what we give Him, and He multiplies it and uses it to bring others to himself. I tell Him every day, "I'm available." How wonderful it is to allow the Holy Spirit to shape the quiet nature of the Peaceful Phlegmatic into one who is available for God.

SHY

Picture a social gathering with people swarming every-where. Invariably there is a shy child, perhaps a demure little girl peeking at the crowd from behind Mom's legs. When we see this child, we think, "Isn't she cute?" We may point out her sweet little face to others, causing her to pull back even more. For adult Peaceful Phlegmatics, this will continue to be reality unless they work at breaking out of their shell. A Peaceful Phlegmatic who has not matured and added balance to her life can be someone who takes no initiative, allowing her life to be controlled by others. To celebrate your Peaceful Phlegmatic personality, find your real interests and pursue them.

Mimi Deeths has seen both the positives and the negatives of being a Peaceful Phlegmatic, and she has worked to find balance, coming full circle.

Growing up as a quiet and somewhat shy Peaceful Phlegmatic was a good place to be in my family. I was the middle child in a family of four brothers. They were a rowdy, restless bunch of guys with boundless energy and a spirit of competitive one-upmanship with each other that resulted in a lot of foolish and funny antics around our house. I loved my funny brothers. They were like a Four Stooges movie playing endless-ly before me, and I was quite content to watch. They were no threat to me, and I did not interfere with their lives unless they asked me to. I considered their requests the supreme flattery. When they had homework they needed help with, girlfriend problems to discuss, money needed for a movie, or minor infractions they needed help covering up, they knew they could come to me for sanctuary. I didn't mind at all for they added a certain spice to my quiet kind of life.

As I grew into my teens I tried to become more like my brothers. I tried to have a vibrant personality; I tried to be wild. I tried to bounce off people the way they did. I failed. I remained the serious, shy, studious, servant type, and I was content with that. I learned as an adult, however, that I was not good at saying no to seemingly endless requests for volunteer help. After marriage and the births of our four children I was a stay-at-home mom in an era where many young moms went back to the workplace. I was the logical choice for filling all sorts of volunteer positions. Somehow, I began believing that the world would stop revolving if I didn't help out. I was not having fun being chairman or volunteer coordinator for everything from the Girl Scout cookie drive to the PTA. I would work too hard—I didn't know how to ask for help, too shy to bother "busy" others, and definitely not assertive enough to speak out.

In many ways I feel as if I have come full circle—from a shy child, to an involved teenager and adult, and then back to a quieter, wiser, and more mature adult. I like doing things for others—it suits me far better than being in charge of others. Looking back, there were definitely times when I could have used a bit more of an outgoing nature. Sometimes I was embarrassed by my shyness and quiet way of accepting things. But God knows the plan He has for each of us, and now I am coming to realize that my quiet acceptance serves me well.

Five years ago I was stunned by the news that I had inoperable cancer. My prognosis was not at all promising. I was never good at talking so I didn't talk about my disease. The doctors talked about it. My husband and grown children talked about it. I slept easily under the influence of morphine. Sleeping, after all, is one of a Peaceful Phlegmatic's greatest moments. The sleep allowed my body to recover from the onslaught of the surgeon's tools. The oncologist felt that since I was relatively young and recovering well, I was a healthy candidate for some experimental treatment. He approached me with his plan. My husband gave his consent. My kids thought it was my best hope. I thought it was great—the people I love most had made my decision for me! All I had to do was follow along.

I have followed their advice for nearly five years now. I have yet to enter the remission phase of my disease, and so I remain on weekly chemotherapy. That's sickening, and it forces me to remain quiet several days each week. But I am moving forward with my life. I am moving forward with discovering more about myself in my quiet retreat. I am finding God because I have time to listen for His voice. I am not shy with Him. He is much like me. I love His Peaceful Phlegmatic, quiet acceptance of who I am!

Notice how both Elaine and Mimi expressed that they had "learned" or "worked" to improve their personality traits. It does take work—no matter what your personality—to overcome our natural traits and mature and become more balanced. As a Peaceful Phlegmatic, take to heart the words of Ephesians 6:19 NCV: "Also pray for me that when I speak, God will give me words. . . ."

All the Personalities include traits that need to be balanced—areas that need improvement, areas where we need to grow. In this chapter we have briefly looked at just a few characteristics of each personality type that tend to get out of balance. Do not use your natural weaknesses as an excuse for immature or poor behavior. Instead, celebrate who God made you to be; celebrate your personality by taking the steps needed to grow and mature in who you are. Ask the Holy Spirit to add those qualities to your life that in the natural sense you may be lacking. When you have this balance and maturity, you truly can celebrate your personality!

Celebrate Your Path

Creating a Tangible Reminder
of Your Purpose in Life

Chapter 5

"I am the Light of the world. So if you follow me, you won't be stumbling through the darkness, for living light will flood your path."

JOHN 8:12 TLB

The material in this chapter was born of one of my speeches. In preparation for my talk, I looked for a Bible verse that addressed the idea of having a mission statement (also called a defining statement, purpose statement, vision statement, personal creed, theme, or slogan for your life). Since my speech outline featured key points beginning with the letter "P," I chose to call this statement a path. I opened my trusty Bible software and searched for verses containing the word "path."

The first verse to come up was Proverbs 5:6 TLB: "She does not know the path to life. She staggers down a crooked trail and doesn't realize where it leads." *Wow! What a perfect verse,* I thought. It even uses the pronoun she. Knowing that you can't just pluck a random verse out of context, I read the surrounding verses. To my disappointment, I learned *she* was a prostitute. *Maybe no one will know the verse's context and I can still use it,* I hoped. *No, I can't do that. Who wants to be compared to a prostitute?*

On second thought, I decided the verse was and still is appropriate for us. When we know God's purpose for our lives but do not follow that path, we are like a prostitute. We take what God has given us and we cheapen His plan by not following that path. Instead, we travel down a crooked trail, not knowing where it leads.

Off the Crooked Path

The dictionary defines path as "a course or manner of conduct, thought or procedure." Where has your life path led? What course are you taking?

Without taking time to intentionally think through our life and its path, we are apt to follow the path of least resistance, allowing the circumstances of life to dictate our direction—and we travel a crooked path. Don Hutcheson, coauthor of *The Lemming Conspiracy: How to Redirect Your Life From Stress to Balance*, says, "Without some kind of personal vision, you have no direction. You follow the herd. And you may not find out until it is too late that the herd is leading you right off the cliff."[1] Amanda Rankin describes it this way:

> I've felt like a golden retriever lying in the middle of a doorway, ready to chase any tennis ball that anyone might throw my way from any room in the house. It wasn't until I was challenged to sit down and write a mission statement, that I really figured out what I

was supposed to DO in life. It brought my life down to a single focus. Now every morning I read my mission statement as a part of my preparation for the day. It sets my tone. I no longer chase the tennis balls of life, but am directed from within.

As Amanda shared, having a mission statement, or knowing your path, empowers you to unify, focus, and control your life. By doing this you are drawing a blueprint or creating a filter though which all of your decisions and activities pass. Lynn Morrissey, who teaches classes on developing mission statements, says her mission statement is "a compass by which I guide my activities and decisions."

Several years ago I was prompted to create what I call a defining statement for my business. Like many who have shared their stories with me, I was listening to a speaker on tape when I heard its catalyst. It was the day my husband and I were moving from Carlsbad to Albuquerque. He was driving the moving van and I was in my car, which was packed to the gills with "stuff," including my fluffy Schnauzer, Tucker. During the five-hour drive I had plenty of time to listen to tapes, replay them if needed, and focus on their content. I don't remember who was speaking, but I do know that God used that person's taped message to bring focus to CLASS. By the time I reached Albuquerque, I was excited with the new vision and purpose I had for CLASS. The statement God gave me is on our business cards and stationery. CLASS is "The complete service agency for both the established and aspiring Christian speaker, author and publisher offering resources, training and promotion." A bit later I redesigned our logo to include a pen and a microphone and the words "speakers," "authors," "resources," "training," and "promotion."

This defining statement didn't change our day-to-day activities, but it did give them focus and clarity. Most importantly for me, the defining statement became a filter for screening new ideas or possible plans. If an idea fits with the mission of CLASS, I look into it further. If it does not, I put it aside or pass the idea onto someone who may be able to use it.

A couple of years ago I got what I think is a great idea: Create cassette tapes people can listen to as they drive through particular areas of New Mexico. Among other things, they'd learn the history of the area and interesting facts about the sights. I won't give any more details because I may want to pursue the idea someday as a side business. Additionally, there's a chance that one of my nephews will attend the University of New Mexico, and it may be something he could pursue during school.

My nature is to get all wound up about a new idea and head off to accomplish the task, forgetting other projects that may be half-finished. Sure enough, when I came up with the idea for travel tapes, I was very excited. I even had a logo and promotional copy all planned out in my head. (Just writing about it is getting my brain whirling again with ideas. I think I need to call my nephew!) However, with the defining statement for CLASS in mind, travel tapes of New Mexico (or any state, for that matter) don't fit. I won't completely drop the idea, but I have put it on a back burner in the hope that it will come to life through my nephew at some later date. This does not make it a bad idea; it's just not the right time or I'm not the one to do it. My business's defining statement helps keep me focused.

> *"Small determined steps, nurtured by a grateful heart and a willing spirit, lead to true success— greater intimacy with God, oneself and others."*
>
> KAREN O'CONNOR, SPEAKER, AUTHOR, AND TRAINER

Another great benefit to defining my business's path is that I can now succinctly answer the question "What do you do?" CLASS is an unusual organization— there's really no other group like us—so I used to simply say I was a speaker and an author, which certainly did not encompass the breadth of our activities.

An article in *Home Office Computing* magazine helped me come up with a more accurate answer. The article suggested measuring your success using several benchmarks. Regarding work habits, it said,

> Have clarity of vision and purpose. When people ask what you do, your answer is an enthusiastic twenty-five words or less—in other words, a mission statement. Don't ever say, "Well, it is hard to explain. It's sort of like . . ." If you have a clear idea of what is unique about your business and how it is positioned in the market, you can sell better. Every decision you make focuses on that vision.[2]

Now when the person sitting next to me on the airplane asks the inevitable question, I have an answer. Offering them my defining statement opens up conversation and often leads to new customers.

Personally Yours

Creating a mission statement makes perfect sense for a business owner. But what about everyone else, from the stay-at-home mom to someone who diligently works a nine-to-five job?

In her book on mission statements, *The Path*, Laurie Beth Jones says, "A personal mission statement acts as both a harness and a sword—harnessing you to what is true about your life, and cutting away all that is false."[3] Indeed, because we are more complex than simply being a wife, mother, or business owner, you may find it helpful to have a specific mission statement for each major area of your life, since knowing where you are going keeps you from traveling a crooked path.

Besides the defining statement for my business, I have one for my personal ministry and for my personal life. Other people have a single mission statement that encompasses all areas of their life. Lynn Morrissey's mission statement is "To glorify God by encouraging my family's and neighbors' spiritual growth by communicating God's love, hope, and truth through speaking, teaching and writing." This one path covers her family and her community, melding her personal and professional life.

The statement I have for my personal speaking and writing ministry is more like a slogan, but it serves me well: "Putting together the pieces of your life within the framework of God's Word." When I look at the books I've written and my speeches, they all fit that statement. I'm not a Bible teacher, per se, but the topics I address all have a biblical foundation—"within the framework of God's Word." And like my business, when I get an idea for a new book or presentation, I run it through my mission statement filter, which is broad enough to allow flexibility but focused enough to give me

> *"We climb the ladder of life one step at a time. With each new rung, the view around us becomes clearer than the year before. What a gift life is."*
>
> FLAVIA WEEDN,
> WRITER AND ILLUSTRATOR

clarity. This statement appears on my ministry business cards and on my speaking information sheets.

Speaker and author Gayle Roper is a firm believer in the value of a mission statement. Hers is "To write quality material that points to the fullness of life in Christ and to teach others to do/find the same." She says of her mission statement,

Such a declaration of purpose keeps you focused on what you believe is your area of calling. Because of my mission statement, I can filter out public relations writing, being secretary of every organization I'm involved in, spending time at colleges as an author-in-residence or teaching junior high English (which I did pre-children). I can also turn down some speaking invitations with a clear conscience.

Gayle was recently asked to set up an editorial service. Remembering that her mission statement says "write" or "teach," but not "edit," it was an easy decision. She gave them a polite no.

If you do not have a business or formal ministry, I encourage you to look at your life as both an enterprise and a ministry. After all, isn't running a household an enterprise? Raising children a ministry? In the next chapter we will look at how to turn passions into an enterprise, but for now, let's move on to creating a personal or family mission statement.

As I prepared to write this chapter, I realized that although I had a defining statement or theme for my professional ventures, I lacked a personal one. Knowing how valuable my professional statements were, I easily saw its importance. So for the last few days I've been mulling this over in my mind, focused on finding a personal mission statement—the path for my personal life.

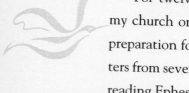

For twelve weeks I've attended a women's Bible study at my church on the book of Ephesians. As part of my personal preparation for the study, I've been reading the assigned chapters from several different versions of the Bible. Last week I was reading Ephesians 5 in *The Message*. I wasn't looking for a personal mission statement, although it had been in the back of my mind. I was simply preparing for the next day's lesson when two verses jumped out. "Observe how Christ loved us. His love is not cautious but extravagant. He didn't love in order to get

something from us but to give everything of himself to us. Love like that" (vv. 1–2).

I instantly knew that my personal mission at this time is to love my husband with extravagance, to give everything of myself. As I cook breakfast or dinner, as I wash the dishes, as I do the laundry—all of these things are something of myself I can give, not expecting anything in return. My husband has had a rough time recently. He is not in a place to be able to give much. But I am. And now I have the Scripture on my bathroom mirror to remind me of my personal mission.

Just after taking on this idea of loving extravagantly, I was put to the test. Chuck has a large radio-controlled model airplane that has been a part of his life for over twenty years. He built it and has too much of himself invested in it to risk flying it. With a five-foot wing span, you can't just tuck it anyplace, so it hangs near the peak of the cathedral ceiling in our family room. With its Red Baron-like decals, it is sure to be noticed. Since it is important to Chuck, I've accepted it as a conversation piece—that it is! It has traveled with us to eight different houses.

A few days ago he took the airplane down to take it to a model airplane show. He spent hours cleaning off accumulated dust that had firmly attached itself to every surface. The plane caused quite a stir at the show and he discovered how valuable it really is. Before Chuck put it back on its hook, he wanted to protect it, so he covered the body and wings with plastic dry cleaning bags—bright yellow advertising and all.

I like my home to look like a showplace, so you can

imagine that even having the airplane there is an act of compromise and love. Having it covered with printed dry cleaning bags went too far. "I'll never be able to entertain again," I wailed.

After my outburst, which I knew was an overreaction, I went outside and trimmed the rosebushes. As I caught my breath, *love extravagantly* came to mind. *Does it really matter if the airplane has bags over it? What's more important, that my husband be happy or that I have a lovely home?* Hmm, that was tough. "Love extravagantly," I told myself. I came back in and apologized—ready to accept the dry cleaning bags. Meanwhile, Chuck had decided I was right and it was really ugly. He had taken the plane down, removed the bags, and wrapped it instead with clear plastic wrap that clung tightly to every curve. It doesn't even show!

Ah, the power of a personal mission statement: to love extravagantly, not cautiously; to give, not to get.

Joann Matthews' family created a family mission statement that was born out of much prayer:

We are godly examples to our family and the body of Christ.

God has made us spiritually and financially rich so that we can bless our families and the body of Christ.

We speak only that which is good for the building up of those who hear it.

We love each other with agape love, therefore we will never rejoice in the iniquity of the other.

We consider and act upon what is right by God's standards and not by what we feel.

We serve the Lord by serving others, therefore our living will not be in vain.

We enjoy each other and the things the Lord has provided for us. Laughing and sounds of joy will fill our home.

Not only did the Matthewses find the creation of their mission statement to be a valuable exercise, they continue to use it for daily guidance. It is posted on the refrigerator, and they often quote it when concluding family prayer time. Joann echoes my encouragement about creating a mission statement for yourself and your family. She welcomes you to use or modify her family's statement until you can write your own.

For many people the thought of creating a mission statement seems daunting. Even Joann Matthews, who helped create her family's mission statement, has struggled to write her own. She's made several starts, but none seem just right. Three years ago

> *"We women can celebrate life because never before has there been such freedom to determine how God wants to use us in tremendous ways. Years ago I couldn't have fulfilled my mission statement to 'Encourage women to know they are Princesses, Daughters of the King.' But today opportunities abound through individual witnessing, speaking, writing, and being involved in secular organizations. The former walls and obstacles have been destroyed. With God's help and direction, we can fulfill every desire God gives us."*
>
> KATHY COLLARD MILLER,
> SPEAKER AND AUTHOR

115

she came close to completing one using a program on Steven Covey's website. Covey also includes information on how to write a personal mission statement in his book *Seven Habits of Highly Effective People*. However, in flipping through the book, I was overwhelmed by the number of charts, graphs, and lists he suggests a person go through. It's a best-selling book, so it must work for some people. Covey himself says it took his family eight months to create their mission statement.

I'm thankful that God dropped my personal mission statement straight into my head. He knows that as a Popular Sanguine, I would never go through all the exercises needed to create something so "official." Yet mine works for me.

Human beings are constantly growing, maturing, and, hopefully, improving. That means our mission statement may change over time as well. Laurie Beth Jones, author of *The Path*, relays the following experience:

> One person asked me, "What if I come up with the wrong mission statement?" When I asked him what his current mission statement was, he didn't have one. I told him, "Well, whatever you come up with will be 100 percent more accurate than the one you have now." I strongly believe that once we set our feet on a path, we will be corrected and guided as long as our hearts stay focused on integrity—both ours and God's.[4]

A Defining Moment

While there are differing ideas as to what a "mission state-ment" actually is and how it is to be used, I want to draw your attention away from what you call your particular statement or path and away from formal processes of creating one. Rather, I hope to inspire you to recognize the value of such a declaration and motivate you to create one, no matter how simple or crude at first.

There is no shortage of entire books, tapes, and other information available about writing a mission statement. For instance, one tape I listened to by Marc LeBlanc was on grow-ing your business. He called his plan a defining statement and said that you needed two "whos" and two "whats" as a part of your statement. Some people I know have followed his formu-la and found it worked.

Laurie Beth Jones suggests a process that includes starting with three verbs, then adding one cause, value, or purpose; and then one group entity or cause. However, especially for start-ing out, I do not believe that our declaration needs to be that structured. If you are the type who plunges into a project 100 percent, you may want to get some books that specifically address the subject of personal mission statements. Personally, I found Laurie Beth Jones' book *The Path* to be the most clear and straightforward.

Advice varies on the subject of mission statements, so I have gathered some basic guidelines to help you think about your life and your path. The goal is to create a tangible reminder of your purpose in life. This is a process of looking back but moving forward. We look back at where we've been and our areas of expertise, then we look forward to our future and where we hope to be. Personal coach Steve Martin calls this your personal constitution: "It takes prayerful introspection, careful analysis and thoughtful expression to produce it in its final form."

I believe that before you can define and celebrate your path, you must know your purpose in life. As we addressed in chapter 3, this is a prayerful process, one that is not apt to happen overnight. If you are clear on your purpose, forming that purpose into a statement that you can read and repeat is a much easier task.

As Christians, we know our general purpose is to glorify and love God—"that I may know Him and the power of His resurrection, and the fellowship of His sufferings, being conformed to His death" (Philippians 3:10 NKJV). He also created us to have a specific mission. As Lynn Morrissey says, "Because Jesus had a God-given mission, He knew exactly why He came to earth and what He was to accomplish. Having a mission kept Him focused, enabled Him to set priorities, and allowed Him to bypass tasks that were not part of God's will for Him. As a result, He perfectly achieved God's assignment in a mere thirty-three years on earth. You, too, have a God-given mission—a 'reason for doing.'" Ephesians 2:10 NKJV tells us, "For we are His workmanship, created in Christ Jesus for good works, which God prepared beforehand that we should walk in them."

God has a purpose for each of us; a path in which we should walk. I claim Psalm 32:8 from *The Living Bible* as my life verse. It says, "I will instruct you (says the Lord) and guide you along the best pathway for your life; I will advise you and watch your progress."

So first, you must know your purpose, at least what it is now since it may change over time. Your personality, as discussed in chapter 4, will also play a role in celebrating your purpose and declaring your path. Laurie Beth Jones says, "Your mission will be perfectly suited to your personality."[5]

Once you have a clear idea about your purpose, you can begin to define it in words. Author Judith Couchman suggests, "Structure your mission statement in terms general enough to span a lifetime, but specific enough to guide your goals and decision-making. State the people you want to reach and the desired outcome of serving them." Sheena Fleener has worked with corporations, churches, and other organizations to help them create mission statements. She advises,

Pray and spend quiet time with the objectives in

> *"Though we will always face obstacles when pursuing our purpose, we have much more freedom than our foremothers did to be our unique selves and influence the world. We can be who God calls us to be, and do what He's asked us to do. And though that's always been His call to women, I think we have more support from people in general. No, the circumstances aren't perfect, but they're more promising."*
>
> JUDITH COUCHMAN,
> SPEAKER AND AUTHOR

119

mind before ever putting a pen in your hand or sitting
at a keyboard. Then, sit down and let everything flow
onto the paper. It's real important at this point to let
God write anything through you that He wants: do not
edit out anything! Even if something sounds funny or
far-fetched, write it down. Then put it away for at least
twenty-four hours. Pray about it some more. Then
share it with others asking for additions, deletions, or
comments (checking your feelings at the door). Then
take all the input and ask God what He wants the final
outcome to be. Be ready to be flexible if you see that
your mission statement needs tweaking later on.

Certainly in my life, and in creating a tangible reminder of
my purpose in life, I have found prayer to be a more vital aspect
of developing my path than any set formula.

Amanda Rankin describes her creative process this way:

It started out on a long page, and over a period of
about a month, I was able to distill it down into one
paragraph. I started out with several statements going
several different directions, but as the Bible says, "A
double-minded man is unstable in all his ways."
Eventually, through prayer and looking at my
Personality profile, I brought my life down into a single focus.

Creating your mission statement is an individual process.

In fact, some people advise that you choose your words carefully and make sure that they are your own, not borrowed from someone else's well-constructed statement. However, like every rule, there are exceptions.

Joann Matthews hasn't finished her official mission statement, but she has claimed a theme for this year. "I have decided to review my theme each year and if I don't find a better one, I'll stick with the one from the previous year." This year's theme was found on the Internet: "Work like I don't need the money. Love like I have never been hurt. Dance like no one is watching." Here's how this theme has played out in her life:

> I am currently working out of my home. If it was about the money, I would have stayed in my corporate job where I was successful and rising. So, indeed, I'm working like I don't need the money even though I do. My passion is to help see to it that entrepreneurs who have great ideas bring them to pass in successful business ventures. I have taken my strengths and skills from my former career along with my passion and created a home-based business. It's working well. I am available to my family (they love it) and also able to minister in the church as necessary.
>
> Love like I have never been hurt speaks to my relationship building—going outside of myself, my family, my church, and my community to risk new relationships. My goal is to have "real" friends and not just acquaintances and business relationships from

every ethnic group and various cultures.

Dance like no one's watching speaks to my worship of the Lord. I am unapologetically Christian. However, my goal is not to proselytize everyone that I come in contact with. Secure and confident Christians automatically draw people to themselves.

Clearly, finding a simple statement on the Internet is working for Joann.

Like me, Sharon Sanderson found the inspiration for her mission statement while listening to a speaker.

In May of 1994, I attended a CLASSeminar. I knew God wanted me to write a book about my life and how He taught me to trust His heart, but I had no clue what the title would be. I hungered to help hurting people find help and hope in Christ. Trusting God with our pain for His gain was the essence of what I wanted to say.

Florence Littauer helped me come up with the title, *Turning Your Woes to Wows*. So that was it. Five years later, the book is not complete, but God is organizing a ministry from this title. He taught me that He wants to take our wounds of existence (woes) and turn them into wonderful opportunities for witnessing (wows) about the grace of God.

From the pain of my childhood and the struggle with church, my woes, God is creating a ministry. As I prayed and sought His will, I found this Scripture, "Come back to the place of safety, all you prisoners, for there is yet hope! I promise this very day, I will repay you two mercies for each of your woes!" (Zechariah 9:12 NLT).

The mission statement of my ministry and personal life is to: encourage Christians to turn their wounds of existence into wonderful opportunities for witnessing; restore hope and purpose in place of discouragement; connect hope to the hurting; and reconcile divorced people and blended families to God and the local church—all for the glory of God.

Whether you spend months developing your personal mission statement, or God places it in your heart one day; whether it is inspired by a speaker or even this book, do spend time in prayer focused on creating a tangible reminder of your purpose in life. By doing this, you will know the path you should travel, as Terry Fitzgerald Sieck discovered:

I went back to graduate school when I was forty-five and took a course on nonprofit management. The instructor stressed that successful organizations needed to have a mission statement. It seemed to me that if an organization needed a mission statement, I did, too, so I wrote this: "To encourage people in difficult times to have faith and hope."

A few months later when I finished my degree, I

used my mission statement as a test for the jobs I sought. One friend suggested I go into a retail business with her, but that didn't fit my mission statement. Another thought I should return to work in local government, but that didn't fit my mission statement. I finally took a position with a charity serving people with developmental disabilities. Working with the consumers and their families offered the perfect opportunity "to encourage people in difficult times to have faith and hope." I now follow my mission as a Christian writer and speaker.

Not only has my mission statement been a guide in choosing my career and where I spend my time, it has been important in choosing my friends and even my husband. When I started dating Larry I shared my mission and Christian values with him. He, too, had a mission and values, compatible with mine. If he hadn't, I would not have married him! Knowing my mission has made a significant difference in my life.

Like the women you have read about here, you, too, can create a mission statement, defining statement, theme, or path for your life. What you call it and whether you follow a prescribed formula or dream up something fresh is not important. Focus on the purpose God has given you; the things you value and believe in that are endowed within you. Deborah Carter said, "After clarifying my interests, strengths, gifts, and training, the doors that opened were easy ones to walk through for they matched my mission of spreading the good news about Christ and making His love practical in families."

Isaiah 30:21 TLB tells us, "And if you leave God's paths and go astray, you will hear a voice behind you say, 'No, this is the way; walk here.'" What is your path? Where does God want you to walk? Keep a tangible reminder of your purpose in life in front of you like a light that floods your path. Don't travel down a crooked path.

Celebrate Your Passions

Turning Your Talents, Hobbies, and Interests Into an Enterprise

Chapter 6

I've had an entrepreneurial spirit for as long as I can remember. As a young child I even sold drawings to neighbors. Using crayons, I'd scribble my own brand of artwork on the cardboard in my father's folded shirts that came from the cleaners. Then I'd take my drawings to the homes nearby and peddle my art. My best customers were an older couple across the street. They happily gave me twenty-five cents for each original until one time when I insisted they hang the picture while I watched. My mother reports they complained about my crying after they hung my scribbles upside down.

In my preteen years, I actually sold "lots" in a play village to neighborhood children. We all played with Matchbox cars on a mound of dirt that was waiting to be distributed in our yard. The pile was in our yard, so I sold my friends the right to play on it. I opened a bank and exchanged their real money for Monopoly money, which could be used within the make-believe metropolis. Sure, they could

> *"If I had one wish, it would be that every woman could be excited about going to work every day."*
>
> MARSHA JOHNSON EVANS,
> NATIONAL EXECUTIVE DIRECTOR
> OF THE GIRL SCOUTS USA

have played with their cars in their own yards or in the acres of national forest nearby, but they all doled out their dollars to play on my pile.

I was nineteen when I went into business for myself as a color consultant. Doing color analysis and speaking and writing on color, wardrobe, and makeup supported me successfully for eight years until the fad waned and I had to move on. In the ensuing years, though my regular paychecks came from a variety of sources, including working for my parents, I continued to earn side income from speaking engagements.

Today I own the business I developed while working with my parents, and I champion the concept of looking at oneself as an enterprise.

An Enterprising Idea

More than one in three American households today are involved in entrepreneurship.[1]

Some of us fall very naturally into the world of self-employment. We are bursting with entrepreneurial ideas and have the creative energy to see them to fruition. We see self-employment as a means to craft a life with more freedom and control of our time while doing something we love and enjoy. We long for the intangible—that in-the-body satisfaction that comes from doing work we believe we were meant for, turning our talents, hobbies, or interests into an enterprise. Dr. Melinda Garcia, a psychologist who works with women in mid-life, explains, "We have the reality that we have to work, along with the societal thing that says we don't have to work. So therefore, if I work, I should have some kind of job satisfaction."[2]

Others find themselves forced to look into starting their own business due to the changing work force and downsizing. If this is you, your initial reaction may be fear or anxiety. However, as you read on, you may change your perspective and see that opportunities abound.

Research shows that those who run their own business are more satisfied with their work. They're twice as likely as non-owners to be "extremely satisfied" on the job.[3] *Executive Female* magazine reports, "Whether they're downsized, laid off, restructured out of a job or just plain want to jump before they're pushed, women are leaving traditional corporate positions to start home-based businesses in droves."[4]

Even if your job seems secure today, I encourage you to examine your passions and see about using them to build an enterprise of your own, even if on the side for now. *Working Woman* magazine rather harshly reminds us, "The company you're pouring your heart and soul into may shed you at any time, like an unsightly bit of lint."[5]

Perhaps at this point in your life being home with your children is your highest priority. You are to be applauded.

> "If I feel full, then my life flows into all kinds of worthwhile projects I want to do. But if I am doing them only because I think I should, it becomes very draining. To me the idea of balance is making sure that you don't just work all the time, that you have down time."
>
> JILL EIKENBERRY,
> FILM AND STAGE ACTRESS

However, before you know it the children will be grown. One study reported that 48 percent of stay-at-home moms expect to return to the workplace in the future.[6] Why not take your skills and interests and look into turning them into a home-based business, something that starts small and takes little of your time. Something that will provide additional income while allowing you to keep your priorities in order. Something that may grow as your time and availability grow. Something that will offer you a bit of a safety net should your life take a sudden turn. The U.S. Small Business Administration estimates the number of women-owned businesses almost doubled during the 1990s. Mothers represent the majority of this group, and 60 percent of these businesses started in the home.

The world of work is no longer the well-defined, established entity it used to be. More and more people, especially women, have changed their priorities. We desire more balance and freedom, more creativity and control in our lives.

This shift in attitude gained prominence in the mid-1990s. An article in *Working Woman* magazine accurately captured what many of us feel:

Instinctively, women know there is more to life than work, and more to work than being skilled, successful and well compensated. Perhaps because we are socialized to be jugglers of relationships and responsibilities, we understand that maintaining a complicated but essential balance between work, family, friends and private time creates happiness. In the '70s and

'80s, as women poured into the workplace, the message that we could do it all left many of us exhausted and frustrated. Now that idea seems as antiquated as it does naïve. . . . A happy life is a collaboration between the heart and mind.[7]

What are your passions? What is your heart saying you would like to do?

> "We work hard, we make friends, we do the right things as often as we flawed mortals are able—and, as we find them, we collect, in the secret rooms of our souls, fragments of dreams."
>
> WENDY REID CRISP, AUTHOR
> AND TALK-SHOW HOST

Balance and Freedom/ Creativity and Control

In today's harried world, wouldn't you like more balance and freedom, more creativity and control? That's apparently what most American workers value. When asked what they wanted from their jobs, American workers placed work/life balance above good pay, enjoyment, a secure future, and enjoyable coworkers.[8] Noted management consultant Nancy Austin has no doubt about what people long for. In the past fifteen years she has averaged more than a speech a week for various confabs and conferences throughout the country. When the audience is all women, the question they all ask is "How can I balance everything to have it all?"[9]

Dawn Pion, Jean Butler-Boren, and Heather McRae-Parks wondered the same thing. These three moms, all working in

> *"A job is not a career. I think I started out with a job. It turned into a career and changed my life. A career means long hours, travel frustration and plain hard work, and finally perhaps a realization that you can't have it all."*
>
> BARBARA WALTERS,
> BROADCAST JOURNALIST

the fashion industry, wanted it all: family, career, and time for themselves. But after years of juggling their home and work lives, they concluded it wasn't working. They didn't want to throw away the twenty-plus years of industry experience, but full-time jobs at the office were no longer an option because they wanted to spend more time with their children.

Together the women formed a business that supplies free-lance services to a host of international companies in the action-lifestyle clothing market. Today they are in a position to actually turn down business, working only with people they like. Although they've been financially successful, they agree the biggest benefit is working at home and setting their own schedules. As Heather says, "It's just nice to be home when the school nurse calls to say your daughter is sick." [10]

Liz Dolan was vice president of global marketing at Nike. While she loved her job, she says it was all-consuming and she had no outside life. She couldn't remember the last time she had slept in her own bed! In an article that appeared in *Fast Company* magazine, she says, "To achieve balance in my life, I needed to create more variety. So I quit. Instead of having one big job, I now divide my work time into thirds: business consulting, private service, and creative projects."

Liz is now president of Dolan St. Clair Inc., a marketing company that works with no more than three clients at any one time. She is on the board of governors of a charitable organization and is developing a talk-radio program. For those seeking a change in their lives she advises,

> You don't have to sit on a mountaintop to discover what's right for you. You always know in your heart what you need to do. But you do have to ask yourself if you are willing to make choices. Put yourself in a position where you are making choices about your life, rather than letting other people make those choices for you. That's what balance is all about.[11]

Karen McCarthy's heart broke when her job kept her from taking her son to his first day of nursery school. "I can't do this. I can't miss them growing up," she recalls saying. This wake-up call spurred what has become a successful catering company run out of her home. Karen started out cooking for a couple and later writing a food column for a newspaper. She attended community fairs to give out samples of her treats. The bookings followed. She is able to watch her sons while she cooks. "I like the money," she says. "But what I like most is having the freedom to say it's important to be a recess monitor at my son's school."[12]

As long ago as 1990 *Fortune* magazine reported that good managers were walking away from careers with big companies in search of control over their own lives.[13] Sharon Hadary,

> *"I want to live each day and moment fully. I will aspire to live a balanced life, not despising any of my roles or responsibilities, but doing whatever I do with a whole heart and to the glory of God—whether it is writing a book or wiping a runny nose. This balancing act is not easy, as any woman knows. We have so much to juggle while we try to stay focused on what takes priority at each moment."*
>
> CONNIE NEAL,
> SPEAKER AND AUTHOR

executive director of the National Federation of Women Business Owners, adds, "Many women who leave the corporate world are choosing to work at home. More women are working at home not so much to provide child-care but because they want more control over their lives, more flexibility, more comfort."[14]

LaDonna Massengill began working part time in a travel agency. Over the years her position crept up to full time—so "full time" that the job controlled her life. When her son's school had a Mother's Day program, LaDonna got the time off, but her boss's displeasure came through loud and clear. LaDonna felt guilty for taking the time for personal responsibilities. And as required, she returned to work immediately after the program.

That was the wake-up call LaDonna needed to make a change. She quit her job and started her own travel agency—Hinsbrook Travel. For the next year and a half she tended to her clients' travel needs from her home. During that time she looked for the right storefront location for her business. She wanted something close to home and her kids' school. Now her children go to her office every day after school. They have their own "office," complete with a desk for homework and a place for games. They're very excited about going to work with Mom. If a child is sick, he or she can go to the office and lie down on the sofa. Best of all, if LaDonna wants to attend a school function, it's her decision. She puts a sign on the door stating when she'll return, and she goes. She's in control of her life—not a boss.

Rebecca Ramsey discovered her creative side when she got married. The catalyst wasn't her marriage, it was the wedding itself. Rebecca had been studying for her coroner's test and doing autopsies when her life took a whole different direction. In planning and preparing for her wedding, she was appalled at the high cost of everything and the difficulty of finding exactly what she wanted. But that experience also awakened in her an excitement for weddings and wedding planning. She changed her course. Rebecca now runs Planned to Perfection out of her home near Albuquerque. She works with brides, planning their wedding and helping them locate the perfect dress—at wholesale prices!

> "Creativity is inventing, experimenting, growing, taking risks, breaking rules, making mistakes, and having fun."
>
> MARY LOU COOK,
> ENVIRONMENTALIST AND
> EDUCATOR

University of Southern California professor William Gartner sums up the issue of balance by saying, "One of the greatest lies of organizational life is that jobs can be as big as the people who fill them. It is not true. Teams can never be as big as our families. Colleagues can never be as big as our friends. Companies can never be as rich, as wonderful, as the people in them. We are bigger than our organizations. We just are."[15]

The End of the Job

In 1994 a *Fortune* magazine cover announced "The End of the Job" and reported that "the traditional job is becoming a social artifact. Its decline creates unfamiliar risks—and rich opportunities."[16] Carol Kleiman, *Chicago Tribune* syndicated jobs columnist and author of *The Career Coach*, echoes what we have all come to understand: "There's no such thing as job security these days."[17] Authors Alvin and Heidi Toffler refer to this change as "a moment of upheaval, a moment for people to increasingly realize that the system they lived with didn't work." They add, "The future doesn't consist of Fortune 500 companies that run everything."[18]

Debbie Wong started her business, DS Consulting, after burning out as an overworked, underappreciated computer programmer and team leader. She was a single woman who wanted more time in her life to do the things she enjoyed and felt a passion to pursue. After much prayer and discussion with others in the same field, Debbie went into business for herself.

I decided to work only part time in DS Consulting.
I created my position to be a twenty- to thirty-hour a
week job as a home-based computer consultant to the
heath care industry. With newly found "free time," I

started preparation for another "business." This one involved my true passions—writing and speaking. In the spring of 1998, Heart's Desire Ministries was born. So I became the founder of not one but two home-based businesses. DS Consulting serves as my main breadwinner. Heart's Desire serves as my heart-warmer. What a blessing to be able to provide for my financial needs and accomplish my own heart's desires through my own business.

Like Debbie, Gail Showalter was feeling burned out and even physically ill from the unbearable stress of her job—working in public education. In preparation for starting her own business, Gail returned twice to the University of Texas in Austin for a master's in curriculum and instruction plus a certification in deficient vision. Gail is now a consultant and teacher for the visually impaired. She calls her business Seeing U Through. She reports,

I am becoming more successful than I could've imagined. The money is not great, yet. Ha! The insurance is a problem—probably the main problem. The rewards of doing what I believe I was naturally gifted to do far outweigh the problems. I do believe that God honors our stepping out in faith—that there will be a way when we are acting in accordance with His design and our own natural gifts.

"Mompreneurs"

Many women have a small home-based business that allows them to focus first on being a mom. They didn't all intend to go into business for themselves, but their skills and services were in demand. Others carefully planned an enterprise that would meet their family and financial needs. The *Los Angeles Times* calls these moms "mompreneurs," saying they are "motivated by autonomy and family responsibilities, not to mention a chance to make more money and have more flexibility."[19]

Sisters Dawn Heisler and Jill Eaton worked together to create their booming enterprise. When Dawn and her husband decided to leave California and move back to their hometown in the Midwest, it meant big changes in both of their lives. Dawn got a job right away as a high school teacher. Her husband didn't fare so well. He worked as a substitute teacher while looking for a job in his field. Things were going well, with Dawn's sister Jill taking care of their child, until Dawn got pregnant again during that first year teaching.

At first, Dawn planned to simply take a leave of absence since good child-care wasn't an issue. But once her son was born, she knew she didn't want to return to work. And yet with her husband still searching for the right job, her income was needed. During her leave of absence, Dawn and Jill began to use their domestic skills to bake cakes and sew dresses and drapes. Their little business quickly became so busy that Dawn never returned to teaching. One weekend they baked five wedding cakes. They also added Christmas cookies to their product line.

Because wedding plans often change but window sizes rarely do, they found making drapes far less frustrating and less demanding, so they steered their business in that direction.

Dawn and Jill used their skills plus tools and equipment already around the house to build a successful business with minimum investment. "If you have domestic skills, people will pay for them," Dawn says.

Michele vandenHeuvel is a stay-at-home mom who required an entirely different level of planning for her home-based sculpting business.

Michele has been interested in drawing, painting, and other creative outlets, especially sculpting, all her life. As a young, introverted child she entertained herself for hours modeling little animals. "As I grew, the arts 'grew with me,'" says Michele. Drawing and sculpting provided an outlet for expressing herself. In high school and then undergraduate and graduate school, she "unofficially" began using her art as a business by selling her little clay animals to help offset tuition and later rent expenses. Still, she never thought she could actually make a living sculpting.

One day Michele's father, who was fond of taking her to museums and galleries, excitedly handed her a small piece of sculptor's clay (not the potter's clay she had been using). He had been to Shidoni, a foundry in Tesuque, New Mexico, to have one of her clay figures cast. The staff gave him the sculptor's clay, explaining it would make it easier to cast her work in bronze. Michele remembers,

At that point my husband, Michael, and I already had a baby, Ben, our eldest. My life was so busy, and as a new mom, I thought, "How can I undertake starting a new business and make a serious commitment with a child?" But that little ball of clay nagged at me, and before I knew it, I was moving forward. I approached my husband to ask him if he would go with me to the bank to take out a business loan to get the casting process on my initial pieces started. He readily agreed, and before I knew it we were signing the bank papers. The work of starting a business has at times been difficult, but the joy of continuing to create keeps me moving forward.

I need to say that for me, my children and family are number one—always have been and will be. I did not start my business thinking of myself and the "empty nest syndrome." My sculpting is a natural extension of who I am as a person, and blends in perfectly with being a mom. I have been extremely blessed this way, that the two complement each other so well. My family is involved in every aspect of my business ("our" business!). My husband offers me his unending faith, love, and support; my children offer me their wonderful ideas and patience, and my parents are always there encouraging me and sharing my (our) sorrows and joys.

Michele has a studio in her home where she creates life-size, whimsical bronze animal sculptures for parks, zoos, and memorial gardens that make people smile and draw children to touch and enjoy them. Michele is also involved in her children's school activities and local volunteer work. As her own boss, she creates her own schedule. "I could not imagine myself not being a mom and a sculptor," she says.

Many moms are fortunate to be able to stay home with their children, but are looking for something they can do on the side to generate additional income for the family and give them a change of pace. For these moms, established home-based businesses are often a good choice.

Melinda Maley was introduced to Creative Memories, a home photo-scrapbook-creating business, after she left her job to be home with her kids. A friend brought a beautifully crafted photo album to show her during a visit. Reviewing the photos brought tears to their eyes as they reflected on their time together as children. Melinda's enthusiasm spread as she later shared her own albums with her friends. Before long she became a Creative Memories consultant. It was just what she was looking for. She can organize classes and lectures according to her own schedule, while doing something she loves and believes in.

Melinda's business became so successful that it began to take up more time than she wanted to spend. But being her own boss, she simply scaled back the workshops and classes she offered. When the children are older or her income needs an increase, she can put more energy into her business and in turn reap the higher rewards.

You, Inc.—A Personal Portfolio

Whether you are currently employed or are a full-time mom, I hope these stories have piqued your interest in turning your passions into an enterprise. It can be something part time for now, or, if you would like, you can develop a full-blown business plan and charge ahead. Your ideas, time, energy, and needs will influence how you go about building your personal portfolio of skills, or what many people are now calling You, Inc.[20]

As I mentioned in chapter 2, an article in *Executive Female* magazine profoundly impacted the way I've shaped my life. "A Life Worth Living" addressed the thoughts and feelings that so many women have offered in this chapter: "The desire to lead a more whole life couldn't be reconciled with the 60-hour weeks and high stress that a job demanded." To take control of your life, the article suggested we "develop a portfolio of skills and activities, some for sale, some to be given as gifts."[21]

> *"It is easy to work for someone else; all you have to do is show up."*
>
> RITA WARFORD,
> WRITER

Charles Handy, business philosopher and author of *The Age of Unreason* and *The Age of Paradox*, advises, "Rather than work at one company, you take on various projects and cultivate several clients. A graphic designer, for example, may work a few days one week designing a book jacket. Once a week she teaches a graphic design class at a local college. She markets herself, chooses the projects she wants, and adjusts her schedule accordingly. . . . Working women have always had to juggle things. They've always had to get things done without having formal authority or titles. They are more comfortable taking control of their lives."[22]

Fast Company magazine calls the person who creates his or her professional life around a personal portfolio of skills a free agent. "Just as sensible investors would never sink all of their financial capital into one stock, free agents question the wisdom of investing all their human capital in a single employer. Not only is it interesting to have six clients instead of one boss, it may also be safer."[23]

I've developed my own business with a personal "portfolio" in mind. Basically my core skills are in the areas of speaking and writing. So, first, I am a speaker and a writer and I sell those skills to various clients. In addition, I teach others to be speakers and writers through the CLASSeminar. I assist other speakers in getting published through the CLASS Reunion. I organize the Southern California Women's Retreat to help introduce new speakers and launch their careers. Through CLASS, we have a speaker's bureau that helps our CLASSeminar graduates gain access to groups that need speakers. We also have a busy mail order business that features my books, my parents' books, and publications from many of our CLASSeminar teachers, plus a variety of resources for people interested in developing their own speaking and writing skills. My portfolio has a theme of speaking and writing, but it includes many different items.

I recently attended a meeting of our local speakers in Albuquerque. Two of my peers lamented the current sluggishness of their businesses. However, both of them are primarily speakers—without a full portfolio of skills and activities. One has written a couple of self-published books and the other has not. By developing a varied portfolio of skills, I have other areas to fall back on should one do poorly. Of course, I could always start a tour business or fix up houses!

My colleague Susan Titus Osborn has created a similar but noncompeting business to mine. For me, speaking is my first skill. For Susan, it is writing. She directs the Christian Communicator Manuscript Critique Service. I often refer people to Susan's business, and she does the same for me.

For fifteen years Susan has taught at writer's conferences and met with conferees to help them improve their skills. She quickly determined that she couldn't accomplish much in fifteen minutes. So twelve years ago she began her manuscript critiquing service, which now generates half of her personal income. A staff of fourteen editors across the country, all published authors, helps with the critiques and edits about 250 manuscripts a year. Additionally, Susan's portfolio includes doing copy-editing for a number of smaller publishing houses. She has also been an adjunct teacher for three college campuses and has written nineteen books.

Susan says,

I love working at home where I am able to keep

my own hours. If my grandkids want to go to a movie, I can take a couple of hours off. If my husband wants to go to the beach for an extended weekend, I can take manuscripts along and edit on the beach. Plus, it is rewarding every few months to get a "gift" in the mail of a published book and have the author say: "This was made possible by your critique." I am thankful that I can make a living owning my own business, doing what I love, and serving God at the same time.

For me, my independence may be due to my upbringing. My parents always encouraged us to do and be whatever we wanted. While my sister Lauren and I have very different goals, I find it interesting that we have both crafted our professional lives around the portfolio idea. Lauren told me,

From the time I was a little girl, I have always wanted to be a mother. I viewed motherhood as the most important job I could have. Yet I was raised in a strong business environment; I thought like a businesswoman, acted like a businesswoman, and organized like a businesswoman. When the time came for me to become a mother, I welcomed that dream as a reality in my life. My children were my priority. As time went on, I found that much of my focus and conversation revolved around diapers, feeding schedules, sports practices, and music lessons. My math skills seemed dull, as before I could always figure the sales tax in my head and automatically know what change was needed. My vocabulary had lost its luster and my knowledge of current events and economics was waning.

To use her skills and interests, Lauren felt a need to be involved in a professional environment, without neglecting her role as a mother. She analyzed her skills and gifts and saw that she was very project-oriented. She wasn't interested in doing the same kind of job or task day in and day out. Instead, she preferred the challenge of creating something new or making order out of chaos and then handing the completed project over to someone else. Lauren had the perfect mind-set for the portfolio concept.

Lauren is an eager learner. With the help of some friends, she learned the major word processing, graphics, and bookkeeping software programs as they came out. She began doing some manuscript transcription and word processing from home. She designed advertisements and newsletters for her husband's store. And as accounting software became more popular, she found herself setting up systems for her friends' businesses.

"I love being able to organize someone else's mess, train them to keep it up, and then walk away except for minimal follow-up," Lauren says. "I hand a completed project over and then can choose what I want to tackle next." Lauren also has a real estate license and has developed a small client base of customers, specializing in the needs of returning missionaries.

Additionally, she takes on a few graphic design jobs, but all on a project by project basis. She even does some work for me.

Lauren offers this encouragement to women: "The greatest blessing and joy of this type of business is that I am home much of the time and available to my children. With today's societal crises, I am convinced more than ever that I need to be home, nurturing, parenting, and loving my children. After all, that is why I wanted to be a mom in the first place."

Kim Garrison's story of business ownership is one that I personally had a hand in creating. Kim worked for my parents and me when CLASS was based in Southern California. Her main responsibility was managing the publicity service, which scheduled interviews for authors on Christian talk shows across the country. When my parents began to talk about scaling back the company and possibly eliminating the publicity service, Kim proposed to take it over and operate it from her home. Within a few months Kim opened CLASS Promotional Services, an independent division of Christian Leaders, Authors, and Speakers Services.

Today, with the help of a full-time employee, Kim maintains an impressive list of clients in the Christian communications industry. They have carried on the excellent reputation of the CLASS organization and work with prestigious Christian publishing houses and many well-known authors. Kim offers a mix of marketing services to a variety of clients, from individual authors and Christian ministries to small and large publishing houses.

True to the portfolio model, Kim sells some skills and gives

"I love being a woman who is older and wiser than I used to be! This is such a wonderful time to be able to fulfill my passion with enough strength and vigor to make an impact. I have raised my children and no longer have the full responsibilities of home! As a grandmother, I am not relegated to just baking cookies and doting on my grandchildren—although I do both. I can also write books, speak to thousands in person via the radio and I have the option of sharing the truth one on one with a hurting sister. I am not limited to one arena! That is the joy of being a woman who is alive and well today."

JAN SILVIOUS,
SPEAKER AND AUTHOR

others away. As her own boss, she's now able to volunteer regularly at her children's schools, which she had always wanted to do. Another advantage is that she never needs paid day care anymore. Her kids come straight home after school or stay home when school isn't in session. Kim is also using the home-based enterprise to teach her children about business (they often pitch in by stuffing envelopes). Her husband has only positive things to say about the venture, as well, and is proud of Kim's accomplishments. Kim says, "It was scary to become self-employed! I never really wanted to start my own business! But at the time it truly appeared to be the clear leading of God on my life, and I took a step of faith. Now I wouldn't want it any other way."

As I look at my own life, I see that I am surrounded by women who have embraced their passions and developed their own businesses—focused enterprises like Michele's sculpting or Melinda's Creative Memories and those with broad personal portfolios like my sister Lauren or my colleagues Kim and Susan.

One of my best friends owns an eighty-agent real estate company. Another works out of her home developing training programs for dental companies. My bookkeeper does monthly bookkeeping for several small businesses and taxes for individuals and companies, plus she's licensed to represent people in tax audits. She works out of her home and meets with clients at their business places.

I met my graphic artist while taking a class she was teaching. Working out of her home, she designs brochures, teaches, develops websites, and is also working at Intel, where she is gaining additional skills. Even my hairdresser works out of her home. I love the fact that I can call her in the morning and get my hair cut that afternoon. Today more and more women are celebrating their passions by developing their own enterprises.

In encouraging people to "perform solo," management consultant Peter Drucker says, "Jobs are too risky. I call them dangerous liaisons. . . . People want to be more like artists, responsible for a defined project done well if not masterfully. Today's truly ambitious people see themselves not as entrepreneurs but as 'independent professionals.'"[24] *Fortune* magazine advises, "You have to actively manage your career. . . . Everybody has to think of himself as a sort of mobile business."[25]

Get a Life!

Ready to develop your own enterprise? Whether you are a

> *"Do we realize the enormous impact we women have on one another? Within our varying circles of female friends and family we have amazing power to foster love, hope, humor, and spiritual growth. From women in quilting circles to moms watching kids on playgrounds to female executives in boardrooms, it cheers my heart to see women devoted to encouraging each other in this life, which can be so often cold and hard. I fear I would not survive without the cushion of my warm, supportive company of girlfriends."*
>
> BECKY FREEMAN,
> SPEAKER AND AUTHOR

stay-at-home mom, a full-time career woman in search of more control and creativity, or someone who's been forced to make a job change, don't look for a regular job—look for customers!

Developing your own enterprise is indeed exciting, but it is not right for everyone. If it were easy, everyone would be doing it. As you begin to think about performing solo, becoming a free agent, developing a portfolio of skills, or shaping You, Inc., Peter Drucker advises,

First ask yourself, can I take it emotionally? You will have to learn to be on your own. The first three years will be rough. You'll have a terrific lunch with a potential client and you'll never hear from him again. It is not the money that is the crucial resource; it is the ability to survive those first few years of hopeful, promising leads that lead nowhere. If you have the emotional fortitude to last three years, you'll succeed.[26]

Drucker's advice is sound. As I mentioned earlier, being in business for yourself is not for everyone. With my cheering him on, my husband tried it awhile but found it wasn't for him. He missed the fellowship of his peers and wasn't able to withstand the tough times and uncertainty. As I write this, he is working with headhunters and looking for a "regular" job.

Charles Handy says the following three conditions should be present in order for a person to succeed in celebrating their passions by being an independent professional:[27]

1. A *proper selfishness*. Can you take responsibility for yourself and your future? Have a clear view of what you want the future to be and believe that you've got what it takes.

2. A *way of reframing*. Do you have the ability to see things, problems, situations, or people in other ways, to look at them sideways or upside-down; to think of them as opportunities, not problems, as hiccups rather than disasters? Reframing is important because it unlocks problems. It can give a situation a whole new look.

3. A *negative capability*. Do you have an attitude that helps you write off mistakes as experience? Negative capability means being able to live with uncertainties, mysteries, and doubts; living with mistakes and failures without being disheartened or dismayed.

If you can answer yes to these questions, you're ready to proceed. When my husband decided to perform solo, we did not ask these questions. In retrospect, I can see he would have answered no to at least two of the questions.

The next step is to find something you can make or do that

> "It is no sin to attempt and fail. The only sin is not making the attempt."
>
> SuEllen Fried,
> SOCIAL ACTIVIST

other people will pay for. Charles Handy suggests:

Ask ten people you know well what they admire in you. List those qualities, then against each, list two activities in which those qualities have been useful in the past and one type of different activity in which they could conceivably be useful. Ask ten friends to help you do this.[28]

Deborah Lee, a social psychologist and author of *Having It All/Having Enough*, endorses this approach. "It's really important to talk to other people," she says. "That's the only way to find out which issues are internal—which ones are you—and which are the influences around you that make it tough to figure out what you really want."[29]

Another way to find your entrepreneurial calling is to look at what you are drawn to. Larry Smith has led an accomplished and wide-ranging career. He says,

I think there is a sweet spot that each of us has. It's the kind of work we want to perform, the kind that makes us proud. But finding that sweet spot requires deep self-knowledge. You start by looking at what you are drawn to. You try it, you evaluate the experience and you evolve as you discover more about it.

The great thing about being a free agent is that you can correct your course if you find that something isn't working for you. As we mentioned before, Dawn and Jill offered a whole portfolio of skills to various clients—cake-baking, dressmaking, and drapery construction. But as they worked on these passions, they found the stress and urgency of baking wedding cakes and making wedding and bridesmaids' dresses too much, so they made the change and today focus their skills on draperies.

To make a business work, you may need to simplify your life. I left California and moved to a smaller house in New Mexico where the pace of life is slower. Elaine St. James, author of many books on simplicity, including *Living the Simple Life: A Guide to Scaling Down and Enjoying More*, says,

> Simplifying your life is really about gaining control of your life—creating more time, on the job and at home, to do the things you want to do. . . . If you've spent years not knowing what you want to do—in your career, in your family life, with your civic obligations—it can seem like an impossible challenge to figure it out. For many people, it's easier to keep doing what they know they don't want to do, or what they don't mind doing. Simplifying your life frees up time to figure out what really matters.[30]

Some hard self-interrogation may be necessary to determine if being a free agent is right for you. But as you have learned, many women before you have done it.

Your passions may take you in a direction that utilizes your natural skills and abilities but does not need a formal business plan or a loan. Your enterprise may develop slowly, evolving as your time and ability allow.

You may need additional resources. Depending on the particular portfolio skills you are developing, some of the following resources may be helpful to you. They are some of my personal favorites.

- *Fast Company* magazine—You'll note that I quote from this source frequently. It is a big, thick magazine that now comes monthly. Sometimes they stack up until I have the time to get to them. But with every issue I am inspired, motivated, and equipped. To subscribe, call 800/688-1545 or visit their website at www.fastcompany.com.

- *Home Office Computing* magazine—Many of its articles are computer-oriented, but they're geared for the home-based or small business. Additionally, they feature many other articles of interest to the self-employed. Call 800/288-7812 to subscribe or visit their website at www.smalloffice.com.

- www.workingsolo.com/Terri Lonier—This website features an array of information for the person who is working solo. Terri's philosophy is that working solo is not working alone.

- *The Perfect Business* by Michael LeBoeuf—I heard Michael speak to a packed audience at a meeting of the National

Speakers Association. He motivated and inspired me. His book is a good handbook for the person starting his or her home-based business. *The Perfect Business* should be available in your local bookstore's business section.

> *"The only people who never fail are those who never try."*
>
> ILKA CHASE,
> ACTRESS AND WRITER

- *You Can Make Money From Your Hobby* by Martha Campbell Pullen, Ph.D.—From a Christian perspective, this book will guide you through the entire process of building a business by doing what you love. Available through your local Christian bookstore.

- *Your Simple Guide to a Home-Based Business* by Emilie Barnes and Sheri Torelli—Emilie is a master at helping people turn their talents, hobbies, and interests into enterprises. This book is, as it says, a "simple guide" that is a great starting place for the home-based business novice. Available through your local Christian bookstore.

I hope this chapter has both motivated and inspired you to look at your talents, hobbies, and interests, and consider turning them into an enterprise. Reread the stories. Ask yourself the key questions before going into business, and if your heart tells you that becoming an independent professional is the way for you to celebrate your passion, take the necessary steps. I encourage you to start small, do something on the side that doesn't eliminate a necessary income. Continue to educate yourself through books and magazines. Take advantage of the many resources, and learn from others' experiences.

If your business grows and works for your personal life and family, grow with it. If it begins to take up too much time, correct your course. No matter what, celebrate your passions. You've got what it takes!

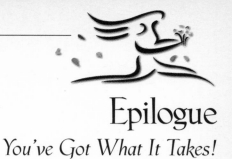

Epilogue
You've Got What It Takes!

"We are women, worthy of His word because He has ordained our lives to be far more than successful— but to be significant on the multi-faceted platforms of our world. I believe we know His calling, our total inadequacy without Him, and the miraculous meaning of our work and lives with Him. Celebrating womanhood!"

NAOMI RHODE, SPEAKER AND AUTHOR

After reading the manuscript for *You've Got What It Takes*, a friend commented, "Some women might not like how you've talked about your accomplishments. They may wish they had your drive and ambition."

I hope you do desire my drive and ambition as they do come from the core principles in this book. The history we have as women makes me excited about who we are today. We do, indeed, have so many opportunities, options, and advantages previous generations did not have. We must celebrate our privileges!

I am propelled, in good times and bad, by knowing God's purpose for my life. Having that solid base and direction gives

"As a little girl my goal was to marry, make a home, and have many children. In the '30s, '40s, and '50s that's what being a woman was.

"I did all that, and then at forty years of age my womanhood changed; my children were late teenagers and in college. I wrote my first book, More Hours in My Day, *and haven't stopped since. Now in my sixties, my view of a woman really hasn't changed—yes; we can do it all, if we keep our perspective and goals toward God.*

"I am presently fighting for my life through cancer, and truly realize all we are and who we are is what we have allowed God to pour into us. I love being a woman, and the difficulties of life merely make us more of a woman!"

EMILIE BARNES,
SPEAKER AND AUTHOR

me complete confidence, even as I continue to grow and change. After writing the final words of the last chapter, I faced tough times and a new turn in my life— one I did not want nor choose. But because I truly know God's purpose for my life, I can ultimately cling to that and count on His direction.

For months I wrestled in my spirit over this crisis. I mentioned my husband's transition. Due to upheaval in his industry, he was forced to seek employment in a neighboring state. I had no desire to move; I love living in New Mexico. My biggest hang-up was my business. I actually like moving, but my business is established. I love it. I have great Christian employees. I couldn't just up and move.

I stopped and asked God what He wanted for my life, His purpose. Hmm . . . put my business first, or my marriage first? You don't need to be a theologian to figure out that one! I believe in God's Word, so I knew my marriage came first—which, in this case, meant accepting Chuck's new job and a possible move of our home and business. God gave me CLASServices, so I believed He would take care of it.

Amazingly, the moment I reached this state of acceptance, my sense of crisis lifted and I was at total peace with the situation. Chuck and I discussed the circumstances at length and agreed it would be foolish to uproot our entire lives until we were sure how things would go in his turbulent industry. For now we will live in two states: I and my dog in our main house near my business in New Mexico; Chuck and his dog in an apartment near his job in Colorado.

> "Today, a woman can be anything she wants to be or do anything she wants to do. I think her greatest opportunity and calling lies in her ability to influence—in her home, her workplace, her church, her world. She sets the tone, carries God's light, and nurtures the vision."
>
> TERRY MEEUWSEN,
> CO-HOST, *THE 700 CLUB*

Today I am writing these words from Chuck's apartment. I have gotten him settled and decorated his temporary home. I have cooked him dinner and left prepared meals in the freezer. Together we are making the best of a difficult situation.

I do not know how long our marriage will be a commuter one, but I do know that God's ways are always best. When I accepted the inevitable and submitted to my husband's needs, my personal crisis turned to total peace. After all, I know God is in control! I know that where I am is where God wants me.

I encourage you to look at your life and the opportunities, options, and advantages you have today. Take the time to get to know God and discover your purpose. This strong foundation—knowing you are where God wants you—will carry you through the inevitable tough times. Understand your personality and its inherent strengths and weaknesses. Grow and mature, finding balance in who God made you to be. Develop your path, a simple statement that defines and helps prioritize the various aspects of your life. Create that tangible reminder of your purpose in life.

When you have taken these steps, celebrating your passion is much easier because you know who you are, what you want, and where you are heading. You've got what it takes!

Appendix
Your Personality Profile

On page 163, in each of the rows of four words across, place an X in the box in front of the one or two words that most often apply to you. Continue through all forty lines. If you are not sure which word "most applies," ask your spouse or a friend, and think of what your answer would have been when you were a child. Use the following word definitions for the most accurate results.

Definitions of Strengths

(1) **Adventurous** One who will take on new and daring enterprises with a determination to master them.

Adaptable Easily fits in and is comfortable in any situation.

Animated Full of life; lively use of hand, arm, and face gestures.

Analytical Likes to examine the parts for their logical and proper relationships.

(2) **Persistent** Sees one project through to its completion before starting another.

Playful Full of fun and good humor.

Persuasive   Convinces through logic and fact rather than charm or power.

Peaceful   Seems undisturbed and tranquil and retreats from any form of strife.

(3) **Submissive**   Easily accepts any other's point of view or desire with little need to assert his own opinion.

Self-sacrificing   Willingly gives up his own personal being for the sake of, or to meet the needs of, others.

Sociable   One who sees being with others as an opportunity to be cute and entertaining rather than as a challenge or business opportunity.

Strong-willed   Determined to have one's own way.

(4) **Considerate**   Having regard for the needs and feelings of others.

Controlled   Has emotional feelings but rarely displays them.

Competitive   Turns every situation, happening, or game into a contest and always plays to win!

Convincing   Can win you over to anything through the sheer charm of her personality.

(5) **Refreshing**   Renews and stimulates or makes others feel good.

Respectful   Treats others with deference, honor, and esteem.

Reserved   Self-restrained in expression of emotion or enthusiasm.

Resourceful   Able to act quickly and effectively in virtually all situations.

Your Personality Profile

Strengths

1. ❏ Adventurous	❏ Adaptable	❏ Animated	❏ Analytical
2. ❏ Persistent	❏ Playful	❏ Persuasive	❏ Peaceful
3. ❏ Submissive	❏ Self-sacrificing	❏ Sociable	❏ Strong-willed
4. ❏ Considerate	❏ Controlled	❏ Competitive	❏ Convincing
5. ❏ Refreshing	❏ Respectful	❏ Reserved	❏ Resourceful
6. ❏ Satisfied	❏ Sensitive	❏ Self-reliant	❏ Spirited
7. ❏ Planner	❏ Patient	❏ Positive	❏ Promoter
8. ❏ Sure	❏ Spontaneous	❏ Scheduled	❏ Shy
9. ❏ Orderly	❏ Obliging	❏ Outspoken	❏ Optimistic
10. ❏ Friendly	❏ Faithful	❏ Funny	❏ Forceful
11. ❏ Daring	❏ Delightful	❏ Diplomatic	❏ Detailed
12. ❏ Cheerful	❏ Consistent	❏ Cultured	❏ Confident
13. ❏ Idealistic	❏ Independent	❏ Inoffensive	❏ Inspiring
14. ❏ Demonstrative	❏ Decisive	❏ Dry Humor	❏ Deep
15. ❏ Mediator	❏ Musical	❏ Mover	❏ Mixes Easily
16. ❏ Thoughtful	❏ Tenacious	❏ Talker	❏ Tolerant
17. ❏ Listener	❏ Loyal	❏ Leader	❏ Lively
18. ❏ Contented	❏ Chief	❏ Chartmaker	❏ Cute
19. ❏ Perfectionist	❏ Pleasant	❏ Productive	❏ Popular
20. ❏ Bouncy	❏ Bold	❏ Behaved	❏ Balanced

Weaknesses

21. ❏ Blank	❏ Bashful	❏ Brassy	❏ Bossy
22. ❏ Undisciplined	❏ Unsympathetic	❏ Unenthusiastic	❏ Unforgiving
23. ❏ Reticent	❏ Resentful	❏ Resistant	❏ Repetitious
24. ❏ Fussy	❏ Fearful	❏ Forgetful	❏ Frank
25. ❏ Impatient	❏ Insecure	❏ Indecisive	❏ Interrupts
26. ❏ Unpopular	❏ Uninvolved	❏ Unpredictable	❏ Unaffectionate
27. ❏ Headstrong	❏ Haphazard	❏ Hard to Please	❏ Hesitant
28. ❏ Plain	❏ Pessimistic	❏ Proud	❏ Permissive
29. ❏ Angers Easily	❏ Aimless	❏ Argumentative	❏ Alienated
30. ❏ Naïve	❏ Negative Attitude	❏ Nervy	❏ Nonchalant
31. ❏ Worrier	❏ Withdrawn	❏ Workaholic	❏ Wants Credit
32. ❏ Too Sensitive	❏ Tactless	❏ Timid	❏ Talkative
33. ❏ Doubtful	❏ Disorganized	❏ Domineering	❏ Depressed
34. ❏ Inconsistent	❏ Introvert	❏ Intolerant	❏ Indifferent
35. ❏ Messy	❏ Moody	❏ Mumbles	❏ Manipulative
36. ❏ Slow	❏ Stubborn	❏ Show-off	❏ Skeptical
37. ❏ Loner	❏ Lords Over Others	❏ Lazy	❏ Loud
38. ❏ Sluggish	❏ Suspicious	❏ Short-tempered	❏ Scatterbrained
39. ❏ Revengeful	❏ Restless	❏ Reluctant	❏ Rash
40. ❏ Compromising	❏ Critical	❏ Crafty	❏ Changeable

(6) **Satisfied**   A person who easily accepts any circumstance or situation.

Sensitive   Intensely cares about others and what happens to them.

Self-reliant   An independent person who can fully rely on her own capabilities, judgment, and resources.

Spirited   Full of life and excitement.

(7) **Planner**   Prefers to work out a detailed arrangement beforehand for the accomplishment of a project or goal and prefers involvement with the planning stages and the finished product rather than the carrying out of the task.

Patient   Unmoved by delay, remains calm and tolerant.

Positive   Knows it will turn out right if she's in charge.

Promoter   Urges or compels others to go along, join, or invest through the charm of her own personality.

(8) **Sure**   Confident, rarely hesitates or wavers.

Spontaneous   Prefers all of life to be impulsive, unpremeditated activity, not restricted by plans.

Scheduled   Makes and lives according to a daily plan; dislikes plans being interrupted.

Shy   Quiet, doesn't easily instigate a conversation.

(9) **Orderly**   Having a methodical, systematic arrangement of things.

Obliging   Accommodating. One who is quick to do it another's way.

Outspoken   Speaks frankly and without reserve.

Optimistic   Sunny disposition. One who convinces self

and others that everything will turn out all right.

(10) **Friendly**   A responder rather than an initiator, seldom starts a conversation.

Faithful   Consistently reliable, steadfast, loyal, and devoted—sometimes beyond reason.

Funny   Sparkling sense of humor that can make virtually any story into a hilarious event.

Forceful   A commanding personality. Someone others would hesitate to take a stand against.

(11) **Daring**   Willing to take risks; fearless, bold.

Delightful   A person who is upbeat and fun to be with.

Diplomatic   Deals with people tactfully, sensitively, and patiently.

Detailed   Does everything in proper order with a clear memory of all the things that happened.

(12) **Cheerful**   Consistently in good spirits. Promotes happiness in others.

Consistent   Stays on an even keel emotionally, responding as one might expect.

Cultured   One whose interests involve both intellectual and artistic pursuits, such as theater, symphony, ballet.

Confident   Self-assured and certain of own ability and success.

(13) **Idealistic**   Visualizes things in their perfect form and has a need to measure up to that standard herself.

Independent   Self-sufficient, self-supporting, self-confident, and seems to have little need of help.

Inoffensive   A person who never says or causes anything unpleasant or objectionable.

Inspiring Encourages others to work, join, or be involved and makes the whole thing fun.

(14) **Demonstrative** Openly expresses emotion, especially affection, and doesn't hesitate to touch others while speaking to them.

Decisive A person with quick, conclusive judgment-making ability.

Dry Humor Exhibits "dry wit," usually one-liners that can be sarcastic in nature.

Deep Intense and often introspective with a distaste for surface conversation and pursuits.

(15) **Mediator** Consistently finds herself in the role of reconciling differences in order to avoid conflict.

Musical Participates in or has a deep appreciation for music; is committed to music as an art form rather than the fun of performance.

Mover Driven by a need to be productive; is a leader whom others follow; finds it difficult to sit still.

Mixes Easily Loves a party and can't wait to meet everyone in the room; no one is a stranger.

(16) **Thoughtful** A considerate person who remembers special occasions and is quick to make a kind gesture.

Tenacious Holds on firmly, stubbornly, and won't let go until the goal is accomplished.

Talker Constantly talking; generally telling funny stories and entertaining everyone; feeling the need to fill the silence in order to make others comfortable.

Tolerant   Easily accepts the thoughts and ways of others without the need to disagree with or change them.

(17) **Listener**   Always seems willing to hear what you have to say.

Loyal   Faithful to a person, ideal, or job, sometimes beyond reason.

Leader   A natural-born director, who is driven to be in charge and often finds it difficult to believe that anyone else can do the job as well.

Lively   Full of life; vigorous, energetic.

(18) **Contented**   Easily satisfied with what she has, rarely envious.

Chief   Commands leadership and expects people to follow.

Chartmaker   Organizes life, tasks, and problem-solving by making lists, forms, or graphs.

Cute   Precious, adorable, center of attention.

(19) **Perfectionist**   Places high standards on herself and often on others, desiring that everything be in proper order at all times.

Pleasant   Easygoing, easy to be around, easy to talk with.

Productive   Must constantly be working or achieving, often finds it very difficult to rest.

Popular   Life of the party and therefore much desired as a party guest.

(20) **Bouncy**   A bubbly, lively personality, full of energy.

Bold   Fearless, daring, forward, unafraid of risk.

Behaved   Consistently desires to conduct herself within the realm of what she feels is proper.

Balanced   Stable, middle-of-the-road personality, not subject to sharp highs or lows.

Definitions of Weaknesses

(21) **Blank**   A person who shows little facial expression or emotion.

Bashful   Shrinks from getting attention, resulting from self-consciousness.

Brassy   Showy, flashy, comes on strong, too loud.

Bossy   Commanding, domineering, sometimes overbearing in adult relationships.

(22) **Undisciplined**   A person whose lack of order permeates almost every area of her life.

Unsympathetic   Finds it difficult to relate to the problems or hurts of others.

Unenthusiastic   Tends to not get excited, often feeling it won't work anyway.

Unforgiving   One who has difficulty forgiving or forgetting a hurt or injustice, apt to hold on to a grudge.

(23) **Reticent**   Struggles against or is unwilling to get involved, especially when such involvement is complex.

Resentful   Often holds ill feelings as a result of real or imagined offenses.

Resistant   Strives, works against, or hesitates to accept any other way but her own.

Repetitious   Retells stories and incidents to entertain you without realizing she has already told the story several times before; is constantly needing something to say.

(24) **Fussy** Insistent over petty matters, calling for a great attention to trivial details.

Fearful Often experiences feelings of deep concern, apprehension, or anxiousness.

Forgetful Lack of memory, which is usually tied to a lack of discipline and not bothering to mentally record things that aren't "fun."

Frank Straightforward, outspoken; doesn't mind telling you exactly what she thinks.

(25) **Impatient** A person who finds it difficult to endure irritation or wait for others.

Insecure One who is apprehensive or lacks confidence.

Indecisive The person who finds it difficult to make any decision at all (not the personality that labors long over each decision in order to make the perfect one).

Interrupts A person who is more of a talker than a listener, who starts speaking without even realizing someone else is already speaking.

(26) **Unpopular** A person whose intensity and demand for perfection can push others away.

Uninvolved Has no desire to listen or become interested in clubs, groups, activities, or other people's lives.

Unpredictable May be ecstatic one moment and down the next, or willing to help but then disappears, or promises to come but forgets to show up.

Unaffectionate Finds it difficult to verbally or physically demonstrate tenderness openly.

(27) **Headstrong**   Insists on having her own way.

Haphazard   Has no consistent way of doing things.

Hard to Please   A person whose standards are set so high that it is difficult to ever satisfy them.

Hesitant   Slow to get moving and hard to get involved.

(28) **Plain**   A middle-of-the-road personality without highs or lows and showing little, if any, emotion.

Pessimistic   While hoping for the best, this person generally sees the down side of a situation first.

Proud   One with great self-esteem who sees herself as always right and the best person for the job.

Permissive   Allows others (including children) to do as they please so as not to be disliked.

(29) **Angers Easily**   One who has a childlike flash-in-the-pan temper that expresses itself in tantrum style and is over and forgotten almost instantly.

Aimless   Not a goal-setter, with little desire to be one.

Argumentative   Incites arguments generally because she feels she is right no matter what the situation may be.

Alienated   Easily feels estranged from others, often because of insecurity or fear that others don't really enjoy her company.

(30) **Naïve**   Simple and childlike perspective, lacking sophistication or comprehension of what the deeper levels of life are really about.

Negative Attitude   One whose attitude is seldom positive and is often able to see only the down or dark side of a situation.

Nervy Full of confidence, fortitude, and sheer guts, often in a negative sense.

Nonchalant Easygoing, unconcerned, indifferent.

(31) **Worrier** Consistently feels uncertain, troubled, or anxious.

Withdrawn A person who pulls back to herself and needs a great deal of alone or isolation time.

Workaholic An aggressive goal-setter who must be constantly productive and feels very guilty when resting. Is not driven by a need for perfection or completion but by a need for accomplishment and reward.

Wants Credit Thrives on the credit or approval of others. As an entertainer, this person feeds on the applause, laughter, and/or acceptance of an audience.

(32) **Too Sensitive** Overly introspective, and easily offended when misunderstood.

Tactless Sometimes expresses herself in a somewhat offensive and inconsiderate way.

Timid Shrinks from difficult situations.

Talkative An entertaining, compulsive talker who finds it difficult to listen.

(33) **Doubtful** Characterized by uncertainty and lack of confidence that something will ever work out.

Disorganized Lack of ability to ever get one's life in order.

Domineering Compulsively takes control of situations and/or people, usually telling others what to do.

Depressed A person who feels down much of the time.

(34) **Inconsistent**   Erratic, contradictory; actions and emotions not based on logic.

Introvert   A person whose thoughts and interests are directed inward; lives within herself.

Intolerant   Appears unable to withstand or accept another's attitudes, point of view, or way of doing things.

Indifferent   A person to whom most things don't matter one way or the other.

(35) **Messy**   Living in a state of disorder, unable to find things.

Moody   Doesn't get very high emotionally, but easily slips into lows, often when feeling unappreciated.

Mumbles   Will talk quietly under the breath when pushed; doesn't bother to speak clearly.

Manipulative   Influences or manages shrewdly or deviously for his own advantage; will get her way somehow.

(36) **Slow**   Doesn't often act or think quickly—too much of a bother.

Stubborn   Determined to exert her own will, not easily persuaded, obstinate.

Show-off   Needs to be the center of attention, wants to be watched.

Skeptical   Disbelieving, questioning motives behind words.

(37) **Loner**   Requires a lot of private time and tends to avoid other people.

Lords Over Others   Doesn't hesitate to let you know

that she is right or that she is in control.

Lazy Evaluates work or activity in terms of how much energy it will take.

Loud A person whose laugh or voice can be heard above others in the room.

(38) **Sluggish** Slow to get started; needs a push to be motivated.

Suspicious Tends to suspect or distrust others or ideas.

Short-tempered Has a demanding, impatience-based anger and a short fuse. Anger is expressed when others are not moving fast enough or have not completed what they have been asked to do.

Scatterbrained Lacks the power of concentration or attention; flighty.

(39) **Revengeful** Knowingly or otherwise holds a grudge and punishes the offender, often by subtly withholding friendship or affection.

Restless Likes constant new activity because it isn't fun to do the same things all the time.

Reluctant Struggles against getting involved or is unwilling to be involved.

Rash May act hastily without thinking things through, generally because of impatience.

(40) **Compromising** Will often relax her position, even when right, in order to avoid conflict.

Critical Constantly evaluating and making judgments, frequently thinking or expressing negative reactions.

Crafty Shrewd. One who can always find a way to get

to her desired end.

Changeable   Has a childlike, short attention span that needs a lot of change and variety to keep her from getting bored.

Personality Scoring Sheet

Transfer all your X's to the corresponding words on the Personality Scoring Sheets, and add up your totals. For example, if you checked Animated on the profile, check it on the scoring sheet. (Note: The words are in different orders on the profile and the scoring sheets.)

Personality Scoring Sheet—Strengths

	Popular Sanguine	Powerful Choleric	Perfect Melancholy	Peaceful Phlegmatic
1.	❏ Animated	❏ Adventurous	❏ Analytical	❏ Adaptable
2.	❏ Playful	❏ Persuasive	❏ Persistent	❏ Peaceful
3.	❏ Sociable	❏ Strong-willed	❏ Self-sacrificing	❏ Submissive
4.	❏ Convincing	❏ Competitive	❏ Considerate	❏ Controlled
5.	❏ Refreshing	❏ Resourceful	❏ Respectful	❏ Reserved
6.	❏ Spirited	❏ Self-reliant	❏ Sensitive	❏ Satisfied
7.	❏ Promoter	❏ Positive	❏ Planner	❏ Patient
8.	❏ Spontaneous	❏ Sure	❏ Scheduled	❏ Shy
9.	❏ Optimistic	❏ Outspoken	❏ Orderly	❏ Obliging
10.	❏ Funny	❏ Forceful	❏ Faithful	❏ Friendly
11.	❏ Delightful	❏ Daring	❏ Detailed	❏ Diplomatic
12.	❏ Cheerful	❏ Confident	❏ Cultured	❏ Consistent
13.	❏ Inspiring	❏ Independent	❏ Idealistic	❏ Inoffensive
14.	❏ Demonstrative	❏ Decisive	❏ Deep	❏ Dry Humor
15.	❏ Mixes Easily	❏ Mover	❏ Musical	❏ Mediator
16.	❏ Talker	❏ Tenacious	❏ Thoughtful	❏ Tolerant
17.	❏ Lively	❏ Leader	❏ Loyal	❏ Listener
18.	❏ Cute	❏ Chief	❏ Chartmaker	❏ Contented
19.	❏ Popular	❏ Productive	❏ Perfectionist	❏ Pleasant
20.	❏ Bouncy	❏ Bold	❏ Behaved	❏ Balanced

Strengths Totals

_____   _____   _____   _____

Personality Scoring Sheet—Weaknesses

Popular Sanguine	Powerful Choleric	Perfect Melancholy	Peaceful Phlegmatic
21. ❑ Brassy	❑ Bossy	❑ Bashful	❑ Blank
22. ❑ Undisciplined	❑ Unsympathetic	❑ Unforgiving	❑ Unenthusiastic
23. ❑ Repetitious	❑ Resistant	❑ Resentful	❑ Reticent
24. ❑ Forgetful	❑ Frank	❑ Fussy	❑ Fearful
25. ❑ Interrupts	❑ Impatient	❑ Insecure	❑ Indecisive
26. ❑ Unpredictable	❑ Unaffectionate	❑ Unpopular	❑ Uninvolved
27. ❑ Haphazard	❑ Headstrong	❑ Hard to Please	❑ Hesitant
28. ❑ Permissive	❑ Proud	❑ Pessimistic	❑ Plain
29. ❑ Angers Easily	❑ Argumentative	❑ Alienated	❑ Aimless
30. ❑ Naïve	❑ Nervy	❑ Negative Attitude	❑ Nonchalant
31. ❑ Wants Credit	❑ Workaholic	❑ Withdrawn	❑ Worrier
32. ❑ Talkative	❑ Tactless	❑ Too Sensitive	❑ Timid
33. ❑ Disorganized	❑ Domineering	❑ Depressed	❑ Doubtful
34. ❑ Inconsistent	❑ Intolerant	❑ Introvert	❑ Indifferent
35. ❑ Messy	❑ Manipulative	❑ Moody	❑ Mumbles
36. ❑ Show-off	❑ Stubborn	❑ Skeptical	❑ Slow
37. ❑ Loud	❑ Lords Over Others	❑ Loner	❑ Lazy
38. ❑ Scatterbrained	❑ Short-tempered	❑ Suspicious	❑ Sluggish
39. ❑ Restless	❑ Rash	❑ Revengeful	❑ Reluctant
40. ❑ Changeable	❑ Crafty	❑ Critical	❑ Compromising

Weaknesses Totals

_____   _____   _____   _____

COMBINED TOTALS

_____   _____   _____   _____

Once you've transferred your answers to the scoring sheet and added up your total number of answers in each of the four columns and your totals from both the strengths and weaknesses sections, you'll know your dominant personality type. You'll also know what combination you are. If, for example, your score is 35 in Powerful Choleric strengths and weaknesses, there's really little question. You're almost all Powerful Choleric. But if your score is, for example, 16 in Powerful Choleric, 14 in Perfect Melancholy, and 5 in each of the others, you're a Powerful Choleric with a strong Perfect Melancholy percentage. You'll also know, of course, your least-dominant type.

Notes

Chapter 1

1. Christian Booksellers Association customer survey (Colorado Springs), 1997.

2. Karen Greenspan, *The Timetable of Women's History* (New York: Simon & Schuster, 1994), 108.

3. Ibid., 166.

4. Ibid., 139.

5. Ibid., 180.

6. Ibid., 189.

7. Lorry Lutz, *Women As Risk-Takers for God* (Grand Rapids, Mich.: Baker Book House, 1997), 16.

8. Christine Lunardini, *What Every American Should Know About Women's History* (Boston: Adams Media, 1997), 32.

9. Ibid., 25.

10. Greenspan, 19.

11. Bolognese jurist Gratian, as quoted in Greenspan, 96.

12. Ibid., 82.

13. Ibid., 32.

14. Lutz, 13.

15. Greenspan, 147.

16. Lutz, 15.

17. Ibid., 20.

18. Greenspan, 38.

19. Lunardini, 9.

20. *Good Morning America* broadcast, 26 January 1999.

21. Greenspan, 80.

22. C. Bernard Ruffin, *Profiles of Faith* (Liquori, Mo.: Liquori Publications, 1997), 166.

23. CBS *This Morning* broadcast, 11 January 1999.

Chapter 2

1. Republican National Committee news release, 8 July 1998.

2. Ginia Bellafante, "Feminism: It's All About Me," *Time* (29 June 1998): 58.

3. Patricia Sellers, "The 50 Most Powerful Women in American Business," *Fortune* (12 October 1998): 80.

4. Janet Bamford and Jennifer Pendleton, "The Top 50 Women-Owned Businesses," *Working Woman* (October 1997): 35.

5. Joline Godfrey, "Been There, Doing That," *Inc.* magazine (March 1996): 21.

6. Stanford Kay, "The Rising Force of the Small-Business World," *Home Office Computing* (May 1996): 20.

7. Bamford and Pendleton, 62.

8. Bellafante, 58.

9. Donna Britt, "Schoolgirl Dreams," *America West* magazine (August 1996): 68.

10. Juliet Schor, "Why (and How) More People are Dropping Out of the Rat Race," *Working Woman* (August 1995): 14.

11. Patti Watts, "A Life Worth Living," *Executive Female* magazine (July/August 1994): 44.
12. "Back to the Future," *Psychology Today* (January/February 1999): 13.
13. Laura Parker, "Too Old? Yeah, Right," *USA Today* (23 October 1998): 1A.
14. Pamela Redmond Satran, "I Don't Feel a Day Over . . ." *Good Housekeeping* (August 1996): 128.
15. Ibid., 87.
16. Ken Walker, "Sure, She's Annointed But Can She Teach?" *Christian Retailing* magazine (5 September 1998): 30.

Chapter 3

1. Frank McCourt, "When You Think of God What Do You See?" *Life* magazine (December 1998): 64.
2. A.W. Tozer, *The Pursuit of God* (Harrisburg, Pa.: Christian Publications, 1993), 78.

Chapter 4

1. *Good Morning America* broadcast, 12 March 1999.
2. Alain L. Sanders, "Would-Be President Elizabeth Dole: The Good and the Bad," *Time Daily News* (4 January 1999), at www.pathfinder.com/time/daily/0,2960,17756,00.html.
3. Time/CNN poll as reported in Bellafante, 58.

Chapter 5

1. Michael Warshaw, "Get a Life," *Fast Company* magazine (June/July 1998): 148.

2. Linda Stein, "How Am I Doing?" *Home Office Computing* (July 1995): 47.

3. Laurie Beth Jones, *The Path* (New York: Hyperion, 1996), xvii.

4. Ibid., 64.

5. Ibid., 25.

Chapter 6

1. Michael Hopkins and Jeffrey Seglin, "Americans at Work," *Inc.* magazine (May 1997): 11.

2. Susan Stiger, "Chuckin' It," *Sage* magazine—a monthly supplement to the *Albuquerque Journal* (November 1996): 10.

3. Hopkins and Seglin, "Americans at Work," 77.

4. Joanne Cleaver, "Corporation to Cottage Industry," *Executive Female* magazine (July/August 1996): 35.

5. Barbara Ehrenreich, "In Search of a Simpler Life," *Working Woman* (December 1995): 28.

6. Bureau of Labor statistics as quoted in *Good Housekeeping* (March 1999): 127.

7. Rosemary Ellis, "Catching Our Balance," *Working Woman* (December 1995): 25.

8. Gemini Consulting and Yankelovich Partners, Workplace Study, as reported in the *Albuquerque Journal* (November 1998): H1.

9. Nancy K. Austin, "What Balance?" *Inc.* magazine (April 1997): 37.

10. Rose Apodaca Jones, "On Their Own Terms," *Los Angeles*

Times (22 January 1999): E1.

11. Anna Muoio, "Balancing Acts," *Fast Company* magazine (February/March 1999): 89.

12. Eva Pomice, "Stay Home, Earn Big Bucks," *Good Housekeeping* (October 1996): 70.

13. Kenneth Labich, "Breaking Away to Go On Your Own," *Fortune* (17 December 1990): 41.

14. Angela Nelson, "Women Increasingly Fill the Ranks of Business Owners," *National Business News* (July/August 1997): 6.

15. Warshaw, 150.

16. William Bridges, "The End of the Job," *Fortune* (19 September 1994): 62.

17. Carol Kleiman, "Those Darn Kids!" *Home Office Computing* (March 1996): 48.

18. Gloria G. Brame, "Seismic Shifts," Working Woman (June 1996): 31.

19. Rose Apodaca Jones, "Own Terms," *Los Angeles Times* (22 January 1999): E4.

20. Amy Saltzman, "You, Inc." *U.S. News and World Report* (28 October 1996): 66.

21. Watts, 46.

22. Ibid.

23. Daniel H. Pink, "Free Agent Nation," *Fast Company* magazine (December/January 1998): 132.

24. Harriet Rubin, "Peter's Principles," *Inc.* magazine (March 1998): 68.

25. Marshall Loeb, "What to Do If a Headhunter Calls,"

Fortune (7 August 1995): 266.

26. Rubin, 68.

27. Adapted from Charles Handy, *The Age of Unreason* (Boston: Harvard Business School Press, 1991), as quoted in Watts, "A Life Worth Living," 81.

28. Ibid.

29. Warshaw, 146.

30. Ibid., 156, 160.